Pupil Book 6

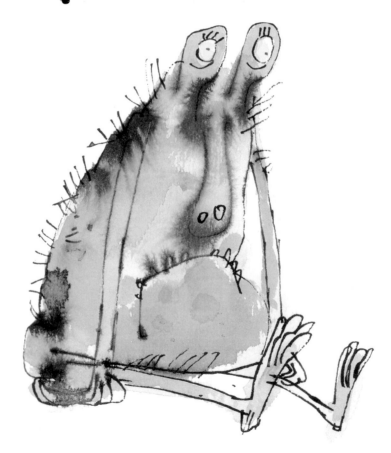

Jonathan Rooke and Karina Law
Series editor: Kay Hiatt

Published by Collins
An imprint of HarperCollins*Publishers*
77–85 Fulham Palace Road
Hammersmith
London
W6 8JB

Text © 2007 Jonathan Rooke and Karina Law
Illustrations and design © HarperCollins*Publishers* Limited 2007

Series editor: Kay Hiatt

10 9 8 7 6 5 4 3 2 1

ISBN 978 0 00 722700 6

Jonathan Rooke and Karina Law assert their moral right to be identified as the authors of this work.

British Library Cataloguing in Publication Data
A Catalogue record for this publication is available from the British Library.

Acknowledgements
The authors and publishers wish to thank the following for permission to use copyright material:
Unit 1: Atheneum Books for Young Readers, an imprint of Simon & Schuster Children's Publishing Division, for the text from *Sea of Trolls* by Nancy Farmer, text © Nancy Farmer, 2004; The Random House Group Limited for the text from *Rescuing Dad* by Pete Johnson, text © Pete Johnson, 2001 (Corgi Yearling, 2001); The Agency (London) Limited for the text from *The Dented Computer*, text © Simon Cheshire, 2003 (first published in *The Oxford Anthology of Mystery Stories*, edited by Dennis Hamley, published by OUP, 2003); Unit 2: Peters, Fraser & Dunlop Limited and Walker Books Limited for the text from *Point Blanc* by Anthony Horowitz, text © Anthony Horowitz 2001; Unit 3: Farrar, Straus and Giroux, LLC, and David Higham Associates for the text from *Boy: Tales of Childhood* by Roald Dahl, text © Roald Dahl 1984; (Jonathan Cape, 1984); Unit 4: "Xmas" by Wes Magee, © Wes Magee, reprinted with kind permission of the author (from *A Fifth Poetry Book* edited by John Foster, Oxford University Press 1986); The Literary Trustees of Walter de la Mare and the Society of Authors as their representative for "Silver" from *The Complete Poems of Walter de la Mare* (1969); Faber and Faber Limited for "Snow and Snow" from *Collected Poems for Children*, text © The Estate of Ted Hughes, 2005; Unit 5: Oxford University Press for the text from *Beowulf* by Kevin Crossley-Holland, text © Kevin Crossley-Holland, 1982, (OUP); Unit 6: *First News* for review of *Sensible Soccer* (XBOX) from *First News*, 9–15 June 2006 © *First News*; screenshot and box front shot © Codemasters; Press Release, Lorna O'Keeffe, Delta Radio; Unit 7: Random House Group Limited and David Higham Associates Limited for the text from *The Suitcase Kid* by Jacqueline Wilson, text © Jacqueline Wilson, 1992 (Random House Children's Books 1992); HarperCollins New York for the text from *The Bad Beginning* by Lemony Snicket, text © Lemony Snicket, 1999; Unit 8: Jon Buscall for *A Good Sport*, printed in *The Guardian*, 28 April 2005, © Jon Buscall 2005, reprinted with the kind permission of the author; Unit 9: The Random House Group for use of "What's in a Name?", "Putting the Boot In" and "Descriptions" by Malorie Blackman, (*Cloudbusting*), text © Oneta Malorie Blackman, 2004 , (Doubleday); Unit 10: Rogers, Coleridge & White for the text from *Maggie's Window* by Marjorie Darke, (*The Oxford Anthology of Mystery Stories*), text © Marjorie Darke, 2003; Unit 11: *The Kent Messenger* 28 September 2006 for *First Walking Bus launched in Sittingbourne*; www.kentwalkingbus.org for *Hop on board the Walking Bus*; Friends of the Earth for extracts from *The Walking Bus: A safe way for children to walk to school*, © Friends of the Earth, 2000; Unit 12: The Orion Publishing Group for the text from *Macbeth* from *Stories from Shakespeare* retold by Geraldine McCaughrean, text © Geraldine McCaughrean, 1994; Samuel French on behalf of the author for the text from *The Railway Children* by Edith Nesbit, adapted by Dave Simpson, text © Dave Simpson, 1987; Unit 14: Marie Curie website, mariecurie.org.uk for text from *The Eiger Challenge*; Sir Ranulph Fiennes for the text of *Sir Ranulph Fiennes' Account*; The Watts Publishing Group Limited for the text from *Nature's Fury: Volcano!* by Anita Ganeri, text © Anita Ganeri, 2006 (Franklin Watts 2006); Unit 15, The Literary Trustees of Walter de la Mare, and the Society of Authors as their representative, for "The Fly" and "Five Eyes" from *The Complete Poems of Walter de la Mare* (1969)

Illustrations: Katherine Baker, Rosalind Hudson, Paul McCaffrey, Brenda McKetty, Kevin Sutherland, Jo Taylor, Martin Ursell, Gwyneth Williamson

Photographs: p19, top: Camera Press, London/Nick Powell; p19, bottom: Camera Press, London, Christopher Simon Sykes; p22, courtesy Stanley Gibbons; p42, top and bottom, Hogs Lodge Hedgehog Sanctuary, Bordon, Hants/Paula Cawley; p53, Almay/Mitch Diamond; p58, www.JohnBirdsall.co.uk; p69, Alamy/Mary Evans Picture Library; p71, Kent Messenger; p73, Kent Messenger; p87, Alamy/Cubolimages srl/Marco Bianchi; p88, Alamy/Adrian Sherrat; p90, Alamy/Eye Ubiquitous/David Clegg; p91, Corbis/Roger Ressmeyer; p 92, USGS/J.D. Griggs; p93, Andrew Grant Reed

Browse the complete Collins catalogue at
www.collinseducation.com

Printed in Hong Kong by Printing Express Ltd

Contents

Fairytales, Fantasy and Beyond

In this unit, you'll find out about features of different fiction genres and write a short story.

In the Dragon's Claws

Jack and Thorgil are two young travellers making a journey to the land of the Troll. Already their Viking warrior companion has been killed in a mighty combat with a troll-bear and they are continuing their terrifying quest alone.

For such a large creature, the dragon was able to float along with scarcely a sound, or at least nothing Jack could hear over the wind and his own laboured breathing. She came up behind them like a leaf coasting on a breeze. Her claws swooped them up before he could even scream.

She did not kill them at once. That would have been too kind. She merely picked them up from the ground and sped off with her talons locked around them like a cage. For a moment Jack couldn't understand what had happened. He was surrounded by black bars – bars that were *hot*. He saw the ground disappear. He felt the wind whistle past his ears.

He heard a terrible, deafening, heart-stopping shriek and recognized it at once. It was the same challenge that had been hurled at Olaf's funeral pyre. "It's the – it's the –" Jack couldn't get the words out. The dizzying ride and his own fear made him sick.

"It's the dragon," Thorgil finished for him. He saw her trying to chip away at the talons with her knife. She was woozy and weak but still attempting to fight.

"It's hot," Jack said. And it was, uncomfortably so. The talons radiated heat, and he had to shift to keep from getting burned. By now they were high above the ground. The dragon flew along, level with the cliffs. Each wing-beat blew a blast of heat past Jack's face, and the dragon's bones creaked mournfully, like a ship under full sail. *It's a* knorr, Jack thought foolishly, echoing Olaf's words from weeks ago: *They call it that because the timbers creak the whole time* – knorr, knorr, knorr. *It takes getting used to.*

The dragon rose and hovered in the air. She opened her talons, and Jack and Thorgil tumbled out into a ring of stone. Around them beady eyes watched intently. Jack realized, with a sick rush of terror, that they had been brought – as a cat might bring mice for her kittens – to teach the dragonlets how to hunt.

"Strike between the chest plates below their necks," Thorgil said in a low voice. "That's what Olaf told me."

Jack could hardly believe his ears. She was up and ready for battle. He was anything but ready. He found himself hypnotized by the dragonlets. They hissed and swayed back and forth, craning their necks. Their eyes were lit with evil intent. How could Thorgil think of fighting now? It was all over. They were doomed.

Four of the monsters – each twice Jack's size – were working up the courage to follow their mother's bidding. The dragon crouched at the side of the nest, making a bubbling noise like a pot of boiling water. Her great, golden eyes were half closed.

from **Sea of Trolls** *by Nancy Farmer*

1 Looking at simple and complex sentences

The author uses a combination of simple and complex sentences to create pace and action. Find examples of this in the passage *In the Dragon's Claws* and make a table. Look at the way each sentence is structured and the words, phrases and punctuation it uses. Note down a comment on the effect it makes.

The first two are done for you.

Simple sentences	Complex sentences
They were doomed.	Jack realized, with a sick rush of terror, that they had been brought – as a cat might bring mice for her kittens – to teach the dragonlets how to hunt.
Comment:	**Comment:**
This is a short, sharp sentence which builds tension. It makes it clear that things are hopeless.	This sentence uses commas and dashes to create two clauses. One clause describes how Jack feels and the other uses a simile which helps the reader picture what is happening. This gives the reader a lot of information fast.

2 Storytelling

What will happen next in *Sea of Trolls*?

With your partner, make up the next part of *Sea of Trolls*. Use the vocabulary and features you'd find in a fantasy book.

Tell the story from Jack's point of view.

Tell the story from Thorgil's point of view.

Tell the story from the dragon's point of view.

Dad's New House

Joe's dad has recently left the family and is living in his new home on his own. Joe has decided he will stay with his father for a while to help him adjust to his new life.

I buzzed on the doorbell, and moments later there was my dad popping out of a house which I'd never even seen before. I can't tell you how weird that was. Perhaps that's why I felt a bit awkward and shy.

Dad smiled nervously. He wasn't sure what to say either. So in the end he said, "Here you are."

To which I replied, "Yeah, here I am," and then felt oddly out of breath. Changing homes really takes it out of you, you know.

Dad stretched out his hand and we shook hands just as if we were meeting for the first time. It was all so peculiar. The whole thing.

"Did your mother bring you?" asked Dad.

"Yeah, her and Claire." Then I added, "They've gone now," just in case he thought they were hiding somewhere.

"Ah, yes," said Dad. "Right."

"So how are you feeling, Dad?"

"Oh, much better thanks," replied Dad firmly. He didn't look much better. He was unshaven with great bags under his eyes and an alarming collection of angry red spots on his face. He had also, I noticed, put on a great deal of weight and now looked as if he had a small rugby ball tucked under his shirt.

"Well, Joe, welcome to my humble abode. I should just warn you, there's not enough room to swing a cat in here."

"It's all right. I've given up swinging cats for the moment."

Dad gave one of his big hearty laughs. "We're going to have fun, aren't we? Well, let's get your bags in. Hey, are all these yours?"

"They certainly are." And I suddenly realized my dad hadn't a clue how long I planned to stay with him.

"And what's in the box?" he asked.

"There's some food and stuff from Mum. Oh yeah, she's put in a packet of your favourite biscuits too."

I think Dad was a tiny bit choked when I told him that, because he looked away from me and muttered, "That was kind of her."

We lugged the bags into the hall which, with Dad and me in it as well, was now looking distinctly crowded.

"We'll leave the bags there for now," said Dad, picking up the box. "And I'll show you the kitchen, which I've just tidied up in your honour."

Dad had certainly cleared the kitchen table of rubbish and the sink was fairly clean too. But the bin under the sink was just brimming over with rubbish. And that is one of Mum's pet hates. She'll say, "Doesn't anyone else notice when the bin is full? Why is it always left to me?" In a certain mood she can talk for ages on this subject. I made a note in my head: must train Dad to empty bins regularly. And on the floor by the bin was a large, dirty tea stain. Something else Mum hates ("All you've got to do is squeeze the tea bags in the sink before throwing them away"). So Dad was going to have to put in some work on the way he handled tea bags as well.

"Well," he said, looking round at the kitchen and then at me. "We're going to make this a half-term to remember, aren't we?"

"Actually, Dad," I said, gently, "half-term finished two weeks ago."

"Did it?" Dad looked astounded.

"Yes, and I'm planning to stay a bit longer than the next few days …"

from **Rescuing Dad** *by Pete Johnson*

8

3 Responding to the text

Answer questions from the , or section.

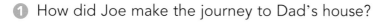

1 How did Joe make the journey to Dad's house?

2 How did Joe feel when Dad opened the door? Why did he feel that way?

3 How did Dad look?

4 How long does Joe want to stay with his dad?

5 Why do you think Joe wants to stay with his dad? What makes you think that?

1 What did Dad look like? What might have caused his appearance?

2 Why might Dad be *choked* when he finds out that Joe's mum has packed his favourite biscuits?

3 What words and phrases indicate that Dad's house is small?

4 What clues are there in the passage about the reasons why Dad has had to move out of the family home and leave Joe's mum?

5 Write a few lines that Dad might write in his diary that night about Joe's arrival at his house.

1 The author describes the way Joe and Dad shake hands when they meet. What does this tell you about their relationship?

2 What is the kitchen like?

3 Why did Joe think that Dad wasn't telling the truth about feeling better?

4 What does *lugged* mean? Why does the author use this verb to show how they moved Joe's bag?

5 What do you think will be Dad's reaction to Joe saying he wants to stay longer than a *few days*? Why will he have that reaction?

4 Drama

In your group of four, make up and act out a scene that takes place after the passage, or a scene that may have led up to the passage, from *Rescuing Dad*.

Think about these questions:

- As well as Joe and Dad, which characters will appear in the scene? What will they be thinking and feeling? What will they say to each other?

- If you choose to act out a scene that occurs after the passage, how will Joe's dilemma be resolved?

5 Storytelling

In pairs, select three cards from the genre pack you've been given.

With your partner, make up a story using all three cards. Rehearse the story and then tell your story to the others in your group.

Tell a fairy story.

Tell a story with a familiar setting.

Tell a fantasy story.

Remember!

- *Use your voice well. Is it the right volume? Is it clear? Do you need to vary the pace?*

- *Make it easy for listeners to create a picture of the setting in their minds.*

- *Give all the information listeners need to understand the story.*

The Adventure of the Dented Computer

Kevin wants to be a detective like his hero, Sherlock Holmes.

OK. I just have to accept it. I'm borderline genius. There are any number of clever kids at St Egbert's School, but I can honestly say, without fear of contradiction, that I'm right up there at the top of the food chain.

My name is Sherlock Holmes. Well, no, actually my name is Kevin, but I'm giving serious thought to having it legally changed. My mum started whimpering and tugging at her collar when I announced my intention, so I think she's OK about it. She's nearly used to the deerstalker hat now.

And it's a *real* deerstalker! A proper one. Exactly like Sherlock Holmes wears.

It was my grandad's. "What d'yer want wi' that dusty old thing?" he said when we found it in his attic. It would have been far too long and complicated to start telling him all about the greatest fictional detective of all time, and how I was destined to be his real-life counterpart. Grandad's not too hot on paying attention. So I said it was for a school project, and he smiled happily and patted my head, and all was fine.

Now then. My first case. It was a classic example of deductive reasoning, which I'm sure even Holmes himself would have been proud of. And a right sinister, nefarious, no-good scheme was at the very heart of this strange and baffling mystery!

I'd been on the lookout for a chance to begin my detective career for ages. I'd read all the Holmes stories twice. Except for a couple of the longer ones. And I'd taped the play versions off Radio 4 and listened to them under the bedclothes at night, so I think that counts.

It started first thing on the Monday morning after half term. We'd had to do an essay over the holiday entitled "An Example of Great Literature". Naturally, I'd written about *The Hound of the Baskervilles*, Holmes's most famous case. Five hundred words, Mrs Womsey had wanted, and I'd done five hundred and twelve! Wayne Banks did "Meka-Robots Comic Summer Special". What a twit. Everyone else did Harry Potter.

Except Thug Robinson. Now, with a nickname like Thug, you can tell he wasn't the sort to go around being nice to small puppies and having tea with the vicar, can't you? He had a scar above his left eye from where he'd fallen off the roof of the toilet block just before Christmas, and if he'd ever bothered to wash his meaty hands you'd have seen the split knuckles he'd got from demanding dinner money with menaces. You didn't want to be in Thug's bad books, unless you enjoyed going to the dentist.

Thug had done *War and Peace.* By some bloke called Toystory, or something.

We all just sat there, silent. Staring at him. I'd seen that book on the bookshelf at home. I think Mum had got it cheap somewhere. Anyway, it wasn't something you actually *read*. It was huge, with tiny print, boring, boring, historical, Russian, boring.

from **The Adventure of the Dented Computer**
by Simon Cheshire

6 Writing a blurb

With a partner, write a blurb for the back cover of *The Adventures of the Dented Computer*.

Remember!

Include:

- a sentence to grab the reader's attention.
- a summary of the plot – but only up to a cliffhanger.
- the exciting and interesting bits of the book.
- some clues about the main characters and the setting.
- quotes from other authors or reviews recommending the book.

7 Independent writing

Plan and write a story of your own in your chosen genre.

Choose a genre for your story (see the boxes on page 13). Read the features in the genre box to help you plan your story.

Fix the genre in your reader's mind when writing your opening. A good way to do this is to make sure that the setting is relevant to the genre. For example, don't describe an alien landscape if your story uses the familiar setting genre.

Remember!

Use:

- strong active verbs to drive the story along.
- a mix of simple and complex sentences for effect.
- descriptions and dialogue to present your characters.

Genre pointers for planning your story

Familiar setting

- Use realistic dialogue and plenty of it.
- Keep the dilemmas clear and understandable.
- Focus on developing one character.
- Use a familiar setting, for example home, school, and only use descriptive words and phrases that add to the story.

Fantasy

- Include magic and fantastical creatures.
- Develop the main character with one or two characters to help him or her along the way.
- Think of a quest.
- Imagine wonderful, "other-worldly" settings.

Fairytale

- Use a narrative voice that feels like someone is telling the story by a fireside!
- Use fairytale phrases.
- Use stock characters, such as princes, princesses or giants.
- Keep the description to a minimum to keep the story moving.

Science fiction

- Include technology.
- Set in the future or on another planet.
- Make the character do something exciting.
- Put the main character in a strange situation.

Mystery

- Include a puzzling crime.
- Include a vital clue for the reader to find.
- Write from the main character's point of view.
- Invent a lively, interesting criminal.

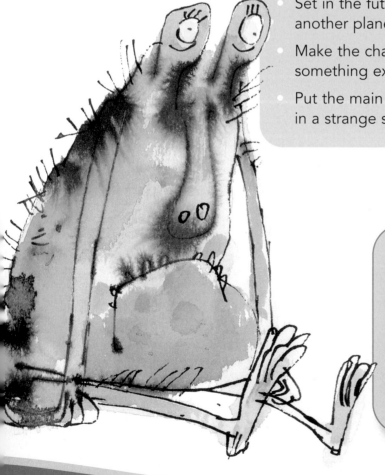

What I have learned

- I can describe and analyse the features of different fiction genres.
- I can select the appropriate features to plan a story in a specific genre.
- I can write and revise a story in a specific fiction genre.

2

Heroes and Villains

In this unit, you'll learn how authors create spy thrillers by using a formula for story and characters, which you'll use to write your own spy thriller.

The Evil Doctor Who Would Rule the World

Alex Rider is a schoolboy spy working for MI6. He has been sent undercover into a castle called Point Blanc. The castle is a boarding school for troublesome boys from the families of the world's rich and famous. Alex is there to spy on the evil headteacher, Dr Grief, and find out what the mysterious Gemini Project is.

The door opened and they went into a huge room that made no sense. Like the rest of the building, its shape was irregular, none of the walls running parallel. The ceiling was about seven metres high, with windows running the whole way and giving an impressive view of the slopes. The room was modern, with soft lighting coming from units concealed in the walls. The furniture was ugly, but not as ugly as the further animal heads on the walls and the zebra skin on the wooden floor. There were three chairs next to a small fireplace. One of them was gold and antique. A man was sitting in it. His head turned as Alex came in.

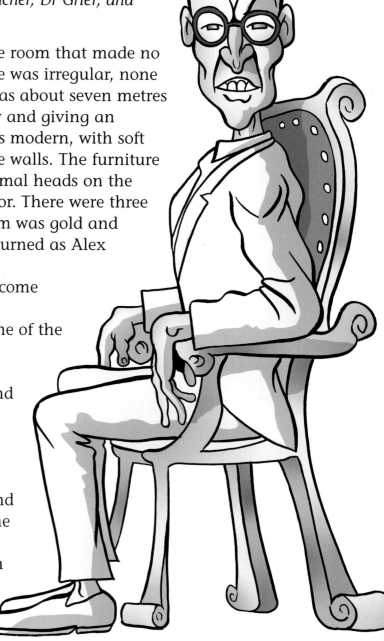

"Good afternoon, Alex," he said. "Please come in and sit down."

Alex sauntered into the room and took one of the chairs. Mrs Stellenbosch sat in the other.

"My name is Grief," the man continued. "Dr Grief. I am very pleased to meet you and to have you here."

Alex stared at the man who was the director of Point Blanc, at the white paper skin and the eyes burning behind the red spectacles. It was like meeting a skeleton and for a moment he was lost for words. Then he recovered. "Nice place," he said.

"Do you think so?" There was no emotion whatsoever in Grief's voice. So far he had moved only his neck.

"This building was designed in 1857 by a Frenchman who was certainly the world's worst architect. This was his only commission. When the first owners moved in, they had him shot."

"There are still quite a few people here with guns." Alex glanced out of the window as another pair of guards walked past.

"Point Blanc is unique," Dr Grief explained. "As you will soon discover, all the boys who have been sent here come from families of great wealth and importance. We have had the sons of emperors and industrialists. Boys like yourself. It follows that we could very easily become a target for terrorists. The guards are therefore here for your protection."

"That's very kind of you." Alex felt he was being too polite. It was time to show this man what sort of person he was meant to be. "But to be honest, I don't really want to be here myself. So if you'll just tell me how I get down into town, maybe I can get the next train home."

"There is no way down into town." Dr Grief lifted a hand to stop Alex interrupting. Alex looked at his long, skeletal fingers and at the eyes glinting red behind the spectacles. The man moved as if every bone in his body had been broken and then put back together again; he seemed both old and young at the same time and somehow not completely human. "The skiing season is over … it's too dangerous now. There is only the helicopter and that will take you from here only when I say so." The hand lowered itself again.

from **Point Blanc** *by Anthony Horowitz*

1 Responding to the text

Answer questions from the , or section.

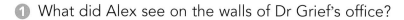

1. What did Alex see on the walls of Dr Grief's office?

2. What was Dr Grief sitting in?
   a) a computer chair
   b) a wheelchair
   c) an antique chair
   d) a deckchair

3. What is unusual about Dr Grief's appearance?

4. Which two words below best describe Dr Grief:
   a) confident
   b) generous
   c) cold
   d) nervous

5. Give examples of words or phrases that make Dr Grief seem creepy.

1. Which word means slow, easy movement?

2. What is Alex's reaction to meeting Dr Grief? Why did he feel this way?

3. How do you think Dr Grief's voice makes Alex feel? Why?

4. Give examples of words or phrases that illustrate Dr Grief's character.

5. Is Dr Grief a good name for a villain? Give reasons for your answer.

6. What do you think Dr Grief is planning to do to Alex?

1. Describe Doctor Grief's emotions. Do they change?

2. When Alex says *Nice place*, what do you think he is thinking?

3. What does Dr Grief say that tells us about his character?

4. Why do you think Dr Grief says *There is no way down into town*? What does it tell you about his plans for Alex?

5. Do you think Dr Grief is a believable character?

2 Role play

Think of three questions you have for Dr Grief and three questions for Alex Rider.

Choose a partner and decide who will take on the role of Dr Grief and the role of Alex Rider. Practise answering each other's questions.

Hotseat as Dr Grief and Alex Rider for the rest of the class.

3 Exciting sentences

Using short, snappy sentences can create pace and excitement in your writing. Authors often use short sentences for action scenes and longer sentences for describing a setting or character.

Make these sentences into shorter sentences to create exciting writing. You can move words around and use more powerful words if you need to.

1 The arctic sharks with razor teeth circled him and he wondered if his stun gun would work in the freezing water. *(Tip: Use a question mark.)*

2 He saw three buttons flashing on the bomb as his palms sweated and then he pushed the red one. *(Tip: Make three short sentences.)*

3 The parachute lines began to snap and he had to think quickly as he headed towards the lake switching on his jet boots. *(Tip: Make four very short sentences.)*

4 The car sped through the empty streets and approached a roadblock so Agent X sped up and headed straight towards it.

5 The snowboard gathered speed as it headed down the mountain and from out of the trees more enemy agents on snow bikes raced towards her and she wondered if the snowboard could out run them.

6 He was terrified but he managed to control his fear and jump from the helicopter with the winch rope between his hands and then he fell at a great speed towards the ice cold sea hoping the winch would slow him down enough.

7 The bullet hole in the space capsule meant that oxygen was being lost and Agent X realised he had seconds to find a space suit and escape but he didn't know where the space suits were kept.

8 Beneath the sheet of ice Agent T swam, protected by her thermal wetsuit, but she knew if she didn't find a hole soon her battery would run out and she would freeze to death and then Dr Fear would destroy the world as we know it.

4 Write your own spy thriller

① *Planning*

First write your plan for a spy thriller. Decide who your characters will be, and what should happen at each stage of the spy plot.

Discuss your plan with a writing partner and listen to their ideas.

② *Drafting*

Start drafting your story. Swap with your partner. Comment on each other's writing with two stars and a wish – a star for two good things, and a wish for one thing you would like to change.

③ *Writing*

Now write your story in full, using your spy plan and feedback from your writing partner.

④ *Checking and editing*

When you have finished, read through again, then make any final changes and check for any mistakes.

What I have learned

- I understand the formula of the spy thriller genre.

- I can plan and write vivid characters.

- I can use a variety of sentences to create suspense and tension.

- I can plan, draft and write my own spy thriller.

Remember!

- Use short, snappy sentences to make action scenes more exciting.

- Provide striking details to give your characters a strong identity.

- Use setting descriptions to create an atmosphere.

- Follow the spy plot formula.

3

This is Your Life

In this unit, you'll read autobiographies and biographies and then write a biography of a person, based on evidence from that person's life.

Boy

The following passage is taken from best-selling author Roald Dahl's autobiography of his life.

By now I am sure you will be wondering why I lay so much emphasis upon school beatings in these pages. The answer is that I cannot help it. All through my school life I was appalled by the fact that masters and senior boys were allowed literally to wound other boys, and sometimes quite severely. I couldn't get over it. I never have got over it. It would, of course, be unfair to suggest that *all* masters were constantly beating the living daylights out of *all* the boys in those days. They weren't. Only a few did so, but that was quite enough to leave a lasting impression of horror upon me. It left another more physical impression on me as well. Even today, whenever I have to sit for any length of time on a hard bench or chair, I begin to feel my heart beating along the old lines that the cane made on my bottom some fifty-five years ago.

There is nothing wrong with a few quick sharp tickles on the rump. They probably do a naughty boy a lot of good. But this Headmaster we were talking about wasn't just tickling you when he took out his cane to deliver a flogging ...

Roald Dahl in the shed at the bottom of the garden, where he wrote his best-selling books

Do you wonder then that this man's behaviour used to puzzle me tremendously? He was an ordinary clergyman at that time as well as being Headmaster, and I would sit in the dim light of the school chapel and listen to him preaching about the Lamb of God and about Mercy and Forgiveness and all the rest of it and my young mind would become totally confused. I knew very well that only the night before this preacher had shown neither Forgiveness nor Mercy in flogging some small boy who had broken the rules.

*from **Boy** by Roald Dahl*

1 Responding to the text

Answer questions from the , or section.

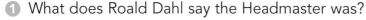

1. What does Roald Dahl say the Headmaster was?
   a) a lamb   b) a clergyman
   c) dim   d) a merciful person

2. What does Roald Dahl feel when he sits on a bench or hard chair for any length of time?

3. Identify one or two words or phrases that Roald Dahl uses to describe the beatings at his school.

4. Find a word or phrase that tells the reader Roald Dahl is remembering his past.

5. What impression does Roald Dahl give of his Headmaster?

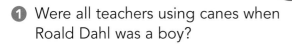

1. Were all teachers using canes when Roald Dahl was a boy?

2. Why was Roald Dahl confused?

3. Why does Roald Dahl use the word *tickling* to describe the use of the cane on children?

4. Why does Roald Dahl choose the word *horror* to describe the impression corporal punishment left on him?

5. Roald Dahl uses the phrase *dim light* to describe the chapel. What effect does this have on the reader?

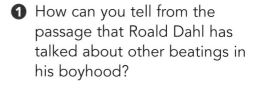

1. How can you tell from the passage that Roald Dahl has talked about other beatings in his boyhood?

2. What is Roald Dahl's view on corporal punishment? Give reasons for your answer by referring to the text.

3. What words or phrases does Roald Dahl use to create the sense he is talking intimately with the reader?

4. In later life, Roald Dahl was not a religious person. Why do you think this was?

5. Were teachers the only people at Repton who beat children?

Looking at a life

Charles Wintergarden was born in 1879. Here are some documents from his life.

CAMBRIDGESHIRE DAILY NEWS
11 November 1918

Biston soldier killed

– Corporal Frederick George Wintergarden, youngest son of Mr and Mrs Thomas Wintergarden and only brother of Charles Wintergarden, Chequers Road, attached to 2nd Battalion Cambridgeshire Light Infantry, was killed in action on 4 November in France on the banks of a French canal.

Summer Term 1890

Biston Elementary School

General:	Charles has worked hard and has done just well enough in the summer examinations, but no more. I fear he has spent too much thought upon his cricket.
English:	Charles has worked with enthusiasm and determination. His written work is the product of an obviously lively imagination, as are some of his excuses for being late in the morning. He reads widely but very often these are penny dreadful comics smuggled in his satchel.
Arithmetic:	Not a natural with numbers and whilst he can add and subtract I am afraid fractions and division are likely to send him screaming from the classroom in sheer frustration were it not for the fact he knows such a spontaneous self dismissal would mean he would miss cricket practice. Tries hard and at the moment it is all I can ask of him as this diligence will pay off in the end.
History:	I very much enjoyed his project on the British in India and I am grateful for his contributions in class, though he must remember the purpose of talking in class is not to keep his friends amused.
Physical Education:	Charles is a good all rounder, light of limb and fleet of foot with a good eye for the ball.

18 January 1900, Africa

Dear Mama and Papa,

Our regiment made it safely to Southern Africa though the sea was rough. I sicked up so much I thought I would lose my stomach.

The Captain says I am good with horses so I am to work in the stables – at first looking after the officers' horses. Suits me. You know how I love horses. It is hot here and dry but perfect weather for cricket and I intend keeping my place in the regimental cricket club – war or no war with the Boer farmers.

Your son, Private Charlie
P.S. Say hello to Constance for me.

Mr and Mrs F. G. Wintergarden,
23, Chequers Road,
Biston,
Cambridgeshire,
England

Marriage Certificate

Marriage at the Parish Church
of St Clement, Biston, in the County of Cambridgeshire

of Charles Anderson Wintergarden of 23, Chequers Road
to Constance Anne Younglove of 14, Rock Mill Lane

Profession of father

Gardener

Bank Clerk

Witnesses   Emily Long
Frederick Wintergarden

I certify this is a true copy.
Rev James Evergreen

Date: 27th day of August 1903

24th August, 1918

France

My dearest Constance,

I miss you so much. I can't wait until this wretched, pointless war is over. I never expected to get called up again by my regiment. They only wanted an old man like me because I can grow food. I work hard each day, organising the young lads in these huge vegetable gardens so we can feed the troops at the front. I watch the young lads marching up to the front and sometimes it makes me weep because I know they won't all be coming back.

Guess what! Last week I bumped into Freddie. "Hello, Little Brother," I said. He was so surprised. But what joy. Here in the middle of France me and Freddie together. We laughed and joked and fooled around so much the other chaps in his platoon wondered at us. But he was alive. It made me glow inside. "Take care," I said to him. But you know Freddie. I was always pulling him out of scraps at school. I wish we were in the same regiment. Then I could keep an eye on him.

Give my love to Dennis and Maisy. Tell them Daddy loves them and to be good. Especially that Dennis – the tinker! Tell him he's not to play his mother up or he'll have me to deal with when I get home.

All my love,

Your husband always,

Charlie

Biston Cricket Club

Membership 1929

Charles Wintergarden
Wicket Keeper

Burials in the Parish of St Clement Biston, in the County of Cambridgeshire in the year 1955

Name	Abode	When Buried	Age	By whom ceremony performed
Charles Anderson Wintergarden	25, Chequers Road	16th May	76	Reverend Alexander Graves

2 Group work

In your group, read the documents about Charles Wintergarden.
List the events of his life on a timeline.

3 Guided writing

You are now going to write a short biography on Charles Wintergarden, based on the documents related to his life.

Think about how you will present the biography. Do you want to present his life in a poster or as a longer piece of writing? Remember to take your audience into account.

Start writing your biography, incorporating important and interesting information you have read in the documents. Read back your lines to yourself to hear what they sound like.

Remember!

- Use all the available evidence to compile the biography.
- Select the most interesting information about the person for the audience.
- Use the past tense and the third person.
- Write the events in chronological order.
- Use time connectives to guide the audience and include key dates.
- Make yourself "invisible" as the author.
- Choose some relevant quotes to include.
- Tell the story from different people's points of view.
- Present some information as text and other information as diagrams, photos and timelines.

4 Think/pair/share

In your pair, read and comment on each other's biographies. Have all the important dates and events in Charles Wintergarden's life been mentioned? Has the information been presented effectively?

What I have learned

- I understand the differences between biography and autobiography.
- I understand how writers select and present information when writing different types of biography.
- I can research, plan and write a biography.

4

The Power of Imagery

In this unit, you'll read and write personification poems by different poets that use imagery, metaphor and simile. Personification is when a writer gives human characteristics to non-human things.

Xmas

Not a twig stirs. The frost-bitten garden
Huddles under a duvet of snow.
Pond, tree, sky and street are granite with cold.
In the house, electronic games warble:
Holly awaits the advent of balloons,
And the TV set glows tipsy with joy.

Wes Magee

Silver

Slowly, silently, now the moon
Walks the night in her silver shoon;
This way, and that, she peers, and sees
Silver fruit upon silver trees;
One by one the casements catch
Her beams beneath the silvery thatch;
Couched in his kennel, like a log,
With paws of silver sleeps the dog;
From their shadowy cote the white breasts peep,
Of doves in a silver-feathered sleep;
A harvest mouse goes scampering by,
With silver claws, and silver eye;
And moveless fish in the water gleam,
By silver reeds in a silver stream.

Walter de la Mare

1 Responding to the texts

Answer questions from the , or section.

1. Name five things that the moon shines over in the poem *Silver*.

2. Find a phrase in *Silver* that suggests that the world watched over by the moon is asleep.

3. Where is *Silver* set? Describe the setting.

4. From *Silver*, which of these statements can you say is **certainly** true?
   a) the dog has paws of silver
   b) the dog is asleep
   c) the dog is crouching

5. For the poem *Xmas* which of these can you say is **certainly** true?
   a) Christmas is over
   b) there is no wind
   c) the garden is keeping warm

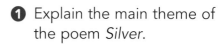

1. Why does Walter de la Mare use the word *silver* many times throughout the poem? What are the effects of this repetition?

2. What do you think Walter de la Mare is describing in these lines?
   One by one the casements catch
   Her beams beneath the silvery thatch.

3. In *Xmas*, why does Wes Magee use the word *duvet*?

4. Give some examples of how, in *Xmas*, the poet chooses words that emphasise the difference between the cold outdoors and the warmth indoors.

5. What impression does Walter de la Mare give of the moon's *character*? Give two reasons to support your answer.

1. Explain the main theme of the poem *Silver*.

2. Find two similarities and two differences between the poems *Xmas* and *Silver*.

3. Explain in your own words why you think Wes Magee chose to describe Christmas using personification.

4. In your opinion, which example of personification is most effective in *Xmas*?

5. What do you think Wes Magee thinks of Christmas? What evidence can you find to support your opinion?

Snow and Snow

Snow is sometimes a she, a soft one.
    Her kiss on your cheek, her finger on your sleeve
In early December, on a warm evening,
    And you turn to meet her, saying "It's snowing!"
      But it is not. And nobody's there.
      Empty and calm is the air.

Sometimes the snow is a he, a sly one.
    Weakly he signs the dry stone with a damp spot.
Waifish he floats and touches the pond and is not.
    Treacherous-beggarly he falters, and taps at the window.
      A little longer he clings to the grass-blade tip
      Getting his grip.

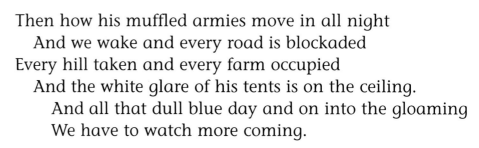

Then how she leans, how furry foxwrap she nestles
    The sky with her warm, and the earth with her softness.
How her lit crowding fairytales sink through the
    space-silence
    To build her palace, till it twinkles in starlight –
      Too frail for a foot
      Or a crumb of soot.

Then how his muffled armies move in all night
    And we wake and every road is blockaded
Every hill taken and every farm occupied
    And the white glare of his tents is on the ceiling.
      And all that dull blue day and on into the gloaming
      We have to watch more coming.

Then everything in the rubbish-heaped world
    Is a bridesmaid at her miracle.
Dunghills and crumbly dark old barns are bowed in the
    chapel of her sparkle,
    The gruesome boggy cellars of the wood
      Are a wedding of lace
      Now taking place.

Ted Hughes

2 Role play

With your partner, describe the pictures in your mind when you read your verse from the poem *Snow and Snow*.

Create a short mime to show the actions of the character.

3 Using active verbs to personify

Poets personify their subjects by using active verbs to describe what they do, for example *huddles*, *awaits*, *peers*.

1 In pairs, think of active verbs and verb phrases to personify two objects that you see when you get ready in the morning, like a toothbrush or a mirror. How would the objects sound, look, move and behave if they were people?

2 Complete the Active Verbs table on PCM 4a.

Subject	Sounds	Looks	Moves	Behaves
alarm clock	screams screeches yells orders shrieks	glares stares	shakes nudges jumps up and down pokes	pesters bullies annoys seeks attention
mirror				
toothbrush				
lunch box				

3 In pairs, create sentences using the subjects and verbs from your Active Verbs table, for example *The alarm clock shrieks and screams*. Follow the instructions on page 30.

Try to make your sentences longer using the conjunctions *and*, *but* and *so*.
For example: *My alarm clock screams **but** I ignore him.*

Improve your sentences by adding further details using the conjunctions *when, whenever, while* or *until*. Try to use the conjunction at the beginning of the sentence and remember to include a comma to separate clauses.
For example: ***When** I ignore my alarm clock's cries, he begins to shake in a rage and scream for my attention.*

Improve your sentences by adding further details using the conjunctions *as, when, whenever, while, until, since, although*.
For example: ***Although** I try to ignore my alarm clock's cries, he shakes and screams **until** I surrender. He has pestered me every morning **since** he moved in.*

4 Paired writing

You are going to write a poem using personification and imagery on the theme of rain. Base your poem on *Snow and Snow*.

Use a skeleton frame to write down your ideas and plan your poem. Each verse should be about a different characteristic of rain.

Write your poem, remembering to check and edit it.

Remember!

- Use active verbs.

- Include colourful adjectives and adverbs.

- Develop ideas using complex sentences.

- Reread and change the order of words to develop a rhythm.

- Include similes and metaphors if you can.

What I have learned

- I can respond to, analyse and compare poetry that uses powerful imagery.

- I can respond to poetry through dialogue and mime.

- I can plan, write and improve an extended poem that uses powerful imagery.

5

A Quest for Adventure

In this unit, you'll read quest stories and find out about their features. You'll construct different reading pathways to explore how authors can shape a quest adventure. Then you'll shape your own quest adventure.

Beowulf

Beowulf was a hero famous for fighting a hideous monster.

As soon as night eased, Beowulf's stallion, one of Hrothgar's gifts, was saddled and bridled. He left Heorot at once, accompanied by the king, his own companions and a large group of Danes.

They followed the monster's tracks through the forest and over the hills. Then they headed into little-known country, wolf-slopes, windswept headlands, perilous ways across boggy moors. They waded through a freezing stream that plunged from beetling crags and rushed seething through a fissure, picked their way along string-thin paths, skirted small lakes where water-demons lived; at last they came to a dismal wood, stiff with hoar-frost, standing on the edge of a precipice.

The lake lay beneath, the lair of Grendel and his gruesome mother. It was blood-stained and troubled. Whipped waves reared up and reached for the sky until the air was misty, and heaven weeped.

The Geats and Danes made their way down to the side of the water. Beowulf braced his shoulders, put on his clinking corslet, and donned his helmet hung with chain-mail to guard his neck.

He dived from the bank into the water, and one of the Geats put a horn to his lips and blew an eager battle-song.

For a whole day Beowulf stroked down through the water. Then Grendel's mother saw him heading for her lair; the sea-wolf rose to meet him, clutched at him, grabbed him, swept him down and into a great vaulted chamber, a hall underwater, untouched by water.

The Geat wrestled free of Grendel's mother; she was coated with her own filth, red-eyed and roaring. He whirled the sword Hrunting, and played terrible war-music on the monster's skull. Grendel's mother roared the louder but Beowulf saw she was unharmed.

from **Beowulf** *by Kevin Crossley-Holland*

1 Responding to the text

Answer questions from the , or section.

1. Who gave Beowulf the stallion?

2. Draw a labelled map of Beowulf's journey.

3. Where was the lair of Grendel's mother?

4. What does *heaven weeped* mean? Why does Kevin Crossley-Holland use these words?

5. What reasons might there be for Beowulf to be scared of Grendel's mother?

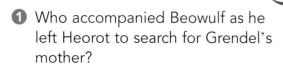

1. Who accompanied Beowulf as he left Heorot to search for Grendel's mother?

2. Where was the *dismal wood*?

3. How does the author show you that the lair of Grendel's mother was a frightening place?

4. What might the companions have been thinking and feeling when Beowulf dived into the water?

5. What sort of enemy was Grendel's mother?

1. Beowulf and his companions pass through wolf-slopes. What do you think *wolf-slopes* are?

2. The author, Kevin Crossley-Holland, tries to develop a sense of place using words. How does he do this and how effective is his technique?

3. What does he mean when he writes *Beowulf played terrible war-music on the monster's skull*?

4. Find at least two other references to sound in this passage. How does this add to the atmosphere?

5. How might Beowulf be feeling at the end of this passage? Give reasons and refer to the passage.

32

2 Grammar work

A non-finite clause is part of a longer sentence. They often start with **verbs** that end in -ing or -ed. For example:

Elated at her rescue, the princess ran into the arms of the knight.

Dragging the monster's head behind him, the hero entered the village.

Copy the sentences below and underline the non-finite clause. Then write two sentences with non-finite clauses of your own.

❶ Clutching the jar of poison, he crept towards the monster's lair.

❷ Gasping for breath, he lifted the giant's sword and plunged it into the monster's heart.

❸ Terrified, he made his way to the cliff edge and dived into the churning sea below.

❹ Pegasus, the winged horse, was far above him, wheeling and prancing among the clouds.

❺ He finally reached the castle, exhausted by the perilous journey.

3 Sentence work

Read the passage below. Rewrite it so it's a richer experience for the reader. To do this you could:

- use stronger vocabulary, for example powerful verbs.

- use interesting adverbs to show the passage of time, for example: *as the darkness thinned.*

- use figurative language like similes and metaphors, for example: *tentacles like iron bars pounding his armour.*

- use a variety of sentences and non-finite clauses, for example: *Sensing danger, he felt panic begin to rise in him.*

- expand the noun phrases, for example change *the beast* to *the terrifying beast.*

 Use words and phrases from the bubbles around the passage to help you, and think of your own words, phrases and sentences.

 Use at least five words from the bubbles around the passage.

poisonous fumes

slayed   perilous

teeth like knives

haze   overjoyed

in the suffocating dark

without warning

twisted roots

his blood ran cold in his veins

screaming

dark chamber

writhing and screaming

lurched

gleaming

The slave knew he was more than his masters had told him as he crept along the passage down into the honeycomb of caves. He felt brave. He was surprised. As he walked in the dark he heard a growl. He saw the beast. He fought him. He beat him. He recovered the three jewels and put them in his sack. He was pleased and returned to the knight who had sent him on the quest who was pleased to see him. He was made into a great knight.

4 Independent writing

Plan a quest adventure story with a choice of reading pathways. Use the flowchart to help you.

Choose a hero, a quest, a menace and a trial. Try to introduce some helpers too.

Remember to work out your ending before you start to write.

> **Introduction: The hero is given the quest.**

> **The start of the quest and the first obstacle.**
> Choice: how will the hero continue the journey?

> **Choice 1**

> **Choice 2**

> **The hero encounters a menace.**
> Choice: what does the hero do to overcome the menace?

> **Trial choice 1**

> **Trial choice 2**

> **Ending: After overcoming the trial, the hero completes the quest and makes their way back to the ordinary world.**

5 Independent writing

Start writing your story by starting your quest adventure in the ordinary world.

- Introduce a character who presents the quest to the hero, and add helpers to help the hero on his journey.

- Give two choices for the journey that the hero can take and follow one through.

- Introduce the menace that stands in the way of the hero's quest, and give two choices for the trial in which the hero faces the menace.

- Describe what happens at the end when they complete the quest.

Remember!

- Choose one hero.

- Follow the pattern of the hero leaving the ordinary world to go to an extraordinary world.

- Know the ending before you start writing and work towards it.

- Give the hero two choices at the journey and trial stages to create different reading pathways.

- Use rich language to develop the setting and atmosphere like Kevin Crossley-Holland.

- Use a variety of sentences, for example sentences containing non-finite clauses.

- Tie the events together with adverbs of time.

What I have learned

- I can identify and explain the features of a quest adventure.

- I understand how to use different reading pathways in my quest adventure.

- I can plan, write and publish a quest adventure of my own.

6

Getting the Facts Straight

In this unit, you'll find out about writing in a journalistic style in print-based and electronic-based forms.

First News 9–15 June, 2006

GAME OF THE WEEK

Sensible Soccer (XBOX)

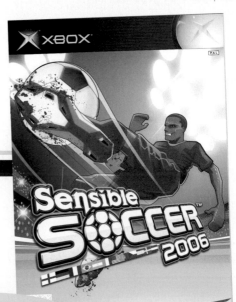

When the original Sensible Soccer game came out years and years ago, it didn't have amazing graphics or anything flash.

Everyone loved it for one reason – it was fun. The fun factor is obviously what they've gone for here, too, with cartoonish players and the option to kit your players out in crazy shorts and dodgy hairdos.

You'll be pretending you're Brazilian with the wicked swerve you can put on the ball, and you can pull off all the usual flair volleys and overhead kicks. Plus there's all kinds of tactics and competitions to get into.

So the big question for Barney – did you have fun playing it?

> Sensible Soccer is like any other football game, but without all of the complicated details, which I really liked. The graphics are funny because it's very cartoony and they have big heads, but that's part of its charm. It's a great game for sleepovers or having mates round.

BARNEY, 12, GAME TESTER

1 Responding to the text

Answer questions from the , or section.

1. When did the original *Sensible Soccer* game come out?

2. Why did gamers like the first version of *Sensible Soccer*?

3. How is *Sensible Soccer* different from other football games?

4. Look at the picture of the packaging for *Sensible Soccer*. Why is it shown in the review?

5. What age of children has the reviewer written for? How do you know from the language chosen?

1. Is this the first version of *Sensible Soccer*? How do you know?

2. What are the positive features of *Sensible Soccer* for gamers?

3. Why does the review include a comment from Barney? What difference does this make to the audience?

4. Do you think the picture of the game screen is a good choice of picture for the review? Explain why you think this.

5. The reviewer uses the word *wicked*. What does *wicked* mean in this review and why does the reviewer use it? Can you find other examples of informal language?

1. Do you think the reviewer thinks this is one of the best games he has reviewed? Explain your answer with reference to the language in the text.

2. How important are the visual parts of this review? Why do you think this is?

3. How has the reviewer used language and sentence structure to make the review seem friendly and personal to the reader?

4. Is this a balanced review? Give reasons for your answer.

5. Is this review aimed at boys or girls, or both? Give reasons for your answer.

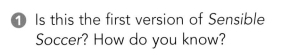

Examining balance in news reports

One of the most famous goals in football World Cup history happened in Mexico in 1986 in a quarterfinal match between England and Argentina. The ball hung in the air just outside the England goalmouth. Argentinean striker Maradona and England's goalkeeper Peter Shilton arrived at the ball at the same time. Maradona used the palm of his hand to push the ball into the goal. Neither the referee nor the linesman saw this foul at the time and the goal was allowed. A few minutes afterwards, Maradona scored one of the greatest ever World Cup goals.

Sports Report A

The story from *The Times* 23 June 1986:

Maradona puts England out of World Cup

England went out of the World Cup yesterday when Diego Maradona scored twice to give Argentina a 2–1 victory in their quarterfinal tie in Mexico City.

Gary Lineker scored his sixth goal in the finals for England in the 80th minute after a fine cross from substitute John Barnes but the equalizer would not come.

Maradona's opening goal in the 52nd minute was controversial because the Argentinean striker, who plays for Napoli in Italy, appeared to be both offside and also to use his arm to flick the ball past Peter Shilton, the England goalkeeper.

But there was no disputing his second four minutes later. A solo run past five defenders ended with him sending Shilton the wrong way and then flicking the ball into the net for the most spectacular goal so far of the 24-nation tournament.

Bobby Robson, the England manager, said after the game: "We were beaten by one goal that was dubious and another that was a miracle.

"We can hold our heads up high. We lost to a very good team."

Sports Report B

A trainee journalist's report:

England beaten fair and square

Argentina won a stunning 2–1 victory over a disappointing England side in Mexico last night.

The victorious Argentinean players will go on to play in the 1986 World Cup semifinals and I think that it was a fair goal.

Diego Maradona, without doubt the greatest football player in the world, scored two fantastic goals within minutes of each other.

Shortly after letting Argentina score the first goal, England's disheartened players could only stand and stare in admiration as Maradona weaved his way through the disorganised English defence to hammer home a goal of glittering brilliance. It was surely one of the greatest goals of this tournament from a magnificent player.

Some fans thought the first goal might not have been a fair goal but anyone can see the ref knew what he was doing.

Paul Brasnet, 12, said, "It was a brilliant goal. The ref was good."

John Barnes was quite good at the end with Lineker but I thought Maradona was better.

2 Read/pair/share

Read the versions of the same story printed on the previous page. Sports report A is a real report printed the day after the match. Sports report B is one a trainee journalist might have written.

Discuss these questions with your partner:

1. Are both reports balanced? Look for:
   - giving both sides of the story
   - using language which is exaggerated or unfair
   - a fair selection of information. Is anything left out or left to the end?
   - presenting journalists' opinions.

2. Why would an editor *not* print the trainee journalist's story?

3. What advice would you give the trainee journalist who wrote the second article?

3 Grammar work

Journalistic writing can use what people say to develop a story. It's often written as reported speech. Look at the difference between reported speech and direct speech.

Direct speech   The policeman said, "You need to come to the police station."

Reported speech   The policeman told the man he would need to come to the police station.

Change these sentences to **direct speech**.

1. The football manager said he was disappointed with the score.

2. The fan said that the goal was superb.

3. Owen said he did not like watching TV all day.

4. His mother suggested he went to the park to play football.

5. The injured man asked if he knew the way to the hospital.

Change these sentences to **reported speech**.

1. "Stop it, both of you!" yelled Tim.

2. Priya said, "I can't help it. I am so scared."

3. "I think we should buy a cat," suggested Hannah.

4. Bill said, "That's a good idea."

5. "These mountains are too dangerous," declared my father.

Change **direct speech** to **reported speech**, and **reported speech** to **direct speech**.

1. The criminal snarled, "You may have arrested me but you can't prove anything."

2. Mrs Smith was moaning that the neighbours were just too noisy since they bought their son a set of drums for Christmas.

3. "I think that gang is going to get a big shock," said the detective smugly.

4. The reporter asked why there were so many fouls in the game.

5. "There was a lot of bad feeling in the tunnel between the players before the match," replied the team captain.

Stop press

You have just received this press release.

Press release: Orphaned albino hedgehog – latest arrival at Hogs Lodge Hedgehog Sanctuary, Bordon

Orphaned albino hedgehog arrives at Bordon sanctuary

A young albino hedgehog is the latest patient at Hogs Lodge Hedgehog Sanctuary in Bordon. Hedgehogs are Europe's oldest mammal but sadly all the indications are that they are suddenly declining.

The main threats to hedgehogs are cars, strimmers, slug pellets, loss of habitat, garden obstacles (ponds, netting) and domestic dogs. Baby hedgehogs born in autumn have a very high mortality rate as they cannot find enough food and put on the fat reserves they need for hibernation. These hedgehogs are known as "autumn orphans". Hedgehogs are protected under Schedule 6 of the 1981 Wildlife and Countryside Act. A blond strain of hedgehogs is found on Alderney in the Channel Islands.

Hogs Lodge owner Paula Cawley said:

"We are delighted to welcome our latest arrival. Albino hedgehogs are quite rare. I have never seen one before. He was found half alive in the Alton direction and taken to Amery Farm Vets at Alton. The vet checked him over and treated him with antibiotics and then took him home for the weekend before passing him over to us. His current weight is 375 grams and we are looking to increase the food he eats (young hedgehogs need to be around 450–600g to survive the winter months). He seems to be making a good recovery and we will give him all the attention he needs to get through to spring. Our patron, local councillor and ecologist Adam Carew, suggested we name him Dinsdale after the Monty Python Hedgehog sketch."

4 Write/pair/share

Read the press release on the left. Think of some questions you might ask the interviewee before writing a news report and write them down.

5 Role play

The phones are ringing constantly in the local newsroom. In the local park a large unusual object has been found. A creature from outer space has emerged from the object, which is clearly some sort of spacecraft. It is already communicating with the local people.

Read the responses on pages 43 and 44 by people who witnessed the alien landing.

In your group, take on the roles of the witnesses. Each of you, in turn, should pretend to be a local newspaper journalist. When it's your turn, interview each witness and make notes to help you write your own news report.

Child playing in the park

I was playing on the swings with my friends when I saw this great big streak of light like a rainbow come out the sky towards me. I was terrified so I hid under the slide. There was a screeching noise as it crashed into the football pitch. There was smoke coming out of it. I couldn't work out what it was. I thought it was a helicopter or something. Then the nose started turning and it opened. I was well scared. This huge alien came walking out holding his hand over his eyes. I think he didn't like the sunlight. I wanted to run away but my legs had turned to jelly. He saw me and then just ... well ... he waved. I thought "He can't be that bad if he waves," but I ran all the way home to tell Mum. I don't like to admit it but I cried ... just a bit.

Owen Jones, 10

Teacher

I was getting some tables ready for the school fair when I saw the spaceship land. I ran to the park and I couldn't believe my eyes. There, in our park, was an alien. It was ... I can't describe it ... it was amazing. The alien saw me and waved. I was scared but it was wonderful. I knew then the alien wasn't going to hurt me. I walked over to him and I shook his hand. It felt cold and dry. Then he drew a picture of his planet in the mud. I think it was Mars. This is a fantastic event. I'm going to invite the alien to speak to our children in assembly. They'll have so much to learn from him and I hope we can take our class to visit the spacecraft.

Dan Sims, 32

Local resident

I don't like him. This alien comes from out of nowhere and ruins our park, scaring our children. Why has he come all this way to our community? What does he want from us? I don't think he accidentally turned left at Jupiter and lost his way in space fog. He seems friendly enough now but we don't know if he has got weapons and things on board his spaceship. What if he is here just to scout out the area? Soon there will be hundreds of them. I know the doctor says he is healthy but he may have all sorts of diseases we don't even know about. And all those people from the television and newspapers. I can't drive down to my own shops for television vans and sightseers from all over the country come to look at him. Mark my words, if he stays, it will mean trouble. I say send him back where he came from and let the people in this community get on with our own lives like we always did.

Emily Widgery, 88

Local doctor

I have examined the alien and I can say there are no signs of any illness. However, I think we should be careful. We are dealing with an unknown being from another world and it may present some health threats to humans in the future.

I am hoping to talk to him later about our medicines and I want to find out if he has any knowledge or medicines that can help humans. I am already beginning to learn his language.

Dr Regina Coldfingers, 56

Police Inspector

Eyewitness reports tell us that the spacecraft landed in the local park on Saturday morning between 9 and 9.30. Our officers arrived at the scene after a distressed mother called to say her child had been frightened by a stranger. A patrol car arrived shortly after 9.40 to find what appeared to be an alien sitting on the swings. I ordered in additional police support and a fire appliance because the spacecraft, buried in the football pitch, was smoking. We requested the stranger, who was sitting on a swing waving, to give himself up and he did so without resistance.

Inspector
Kamal Singh, 48

6 Think/pair/share + Independent writing

Gather all your facts about your report.

Think about your audience and choose the facts and details that'll be most important to them.

Use a first line that grabs the audience's interest.

Tell the story succinctly, using everyday language. The report should explain who is involved, what happened, where and when it happened, and why.

Use a short interview section that develops the story. This makes the event more personal and is a good way to keep the interest of the audience.

Give any important information that the audience might need to know at the end, for example website addresses or telephone numbers.

Remember!

- Know the facts. Check the facts. Be accurate.
- Keep it simple. Use everyday language to explain things clearly.
- Tell people about things that are happening now.
- Know who you are talking to.
- Keep the interview simple, concise and punchy.
- Present the report as if you are speaking to just one person.

What I have learned

- I know the features of TV, newspaper and radio news reports and their effect on an audience.
- I understand that journalists should write balanced reports.
- I can plan and write a newspaper report, taking into account my audience and what they need to know.
- I can plan, write and present a radio news report, taking into account my audience and the importance of presentation.

How to Write Like an Author

In this unit, you'll read texts written by two authors and compare their styles of writing. You'll then write a chapter of a story in the style of one of these authors.

I is for Ill

Andy's parents have split up, and she spends alternate weeks in the houses where her mum and dad live with their new partners. She dislikes most of her new relatives. Andy yearns for things to be as they were before. Her constant friend is Radish, a tiny toy rabbit. The chapters are titled alphabetically, like this title.

I always seem to be getting ill nowadays. I get these headaches or sometimes they're tummy-aches or other times it's an ache all over and I'm either much too hot or so cold I'm shivering. It's always worse on Fridays. That's change-over day.

A few Fridays ago I had a bit of a sniffle on Friday morning. I burrowed right under the bedclothes till I got boiling hot and sweaty and then I called Mum, sounding all sad and sore and pathetic.

Mum felt my forehead and gave me a worried cuddle. I knew Katie would tease me later about being a baby but I didn't care. Mum always makes far more fuss of me on Fridays. I clung to her and said I felt really lousy.

"I think you've got flu," said Mum. "Oh dear. Well, you certainly can't do that awful journey to school, not in this state. You'd better stay in bed."

"All by myself?" I said hunching up as small as I could.

Mum hesitated. "Maybe I'd better stay off work."

"Oh Mum, would you?" I said.

"They won't like it. But it can't be helped. You're really not at all well, pet. You'd better stay in bed all weekend."

"What, at Dad's?"

"No, you'll have to stay put here. You're not up to travelling," said Mum firmly.

I started feeling really sick then. I wanted to stay with Mum and have her making a big fuss of me – but I still wanted to go to Dad's too.

But I made the most of that Friday all the same. Katie flounced off, forbidding me in a whisper to touch any of her videos or records – "Or I'll get you later."

I can beat her in a straight fight but she's got all sorts of devious hateful ways of hurting me. She hides my stuff. She scribbles inside my schoolbooks. Once I found poor Radish floating miserably down the loo and I just know Katie threw her there. She had to spend the night in a bowl of disinfectant and she didn't lose the smell for days and days, so that whenever I cuddled her close my eyes stung.

from **The Suitcase Kid** *by Jacqueline Wilson*

1 Responding to the text

Answer the questions from the , or section.

1. Why did Andy burrow under the bedclothes?

2. Andy hunches herself up small as she says to her mum *All by myself*? What effect does this have on Andy's mum?

3. Why did Katie whisper to Andy?

4. Why does Wilson use a short sentence at the end of the paragraph to write *That's change-over day*?

5. Andy is tricking her mum. Why is she doing it? Give reasons for your answer.

1. Andy says *I always seem to be getting ill nowadays*. As fully as you can, give reasons why Andy is often ill. Why should it be worse on Fridays?

2. Write down four things that Katie did to upset or annoy Andy.

3. Give possible reasons why Katie was unkind to Andy.

4. Andy *clung* to her mum when she first sat on the bed with her. Use a thesaurus to make a list of alternative words for *clung* that Wilson could have used. Why do you think she chose this verb rather than any of the others?

5. Andy says she *felt really lousy*. What does *lousy* mean? Why do you think Wilson uses informal words like these?

1 How do you think Andy's mother felt about staying off work?

2 The author has chosen to write using Andy as the narrator. Why has she chosen to do this?

3 What sort of person is Katie? Give reasons for your answer.

4 What might Mum be thinking about Andy?

5 Wilson uses dialogue to tell the reader about the relationship between Andy and her mum. In your opinion, how effective is the author's use of direct speech in the story? Use examples to back up your reasons.

2 Group discussion

In your group, you're going to compare the writing style of Jacqueline Wilson and Lemony Snicket.

Read the openings on page 50. One is written by Jacqueline Wilson, and the other is written by Lemony Snicket.

Use these questions to help you discuss the authors' writing:

• How do the authors hook the reader?

• What sorts of themes do the authors write about?

• What sort of characters do the authors develop?

• Who is talking to the reader and how does it make the reader feel? Why do the authors use different narrative voices?

• How do the different authors use setting?

• What kind of language do they use?

Write a list for each author, noting down the writing techniques that they use.

Openings

When my parents split up they didn't know
what to do with me. My mum wanted me to
go and live with her. My dad wanted me to go
and live with him. I didn't want to go and live
at my mum's new place or my dad's new
place. I wanted to stay living in our old place,
Mulberry Cottage, the three of us together.
Four counting my pet Sylvanian family spotted
rabbit Radish.

   There were all these arguments about who would get custody of me.
I thought they were talking about custard at first. I hate custard
because you can never tell when there's going to be a lump and it
sticks in your throat and makes you shudder.

from The Suitcase Kid *by Jacqueline Wilson*

If you are interested in stories with
happy endings, you would be
better off reading some other
book. In this book, not only is
there no happy ending, there is no
happy beginning and very few
happy things in the middle. This
is because not very many happy
things happened in the lives of
the three Baudelaire youngsters.
Violet, Klaus, and Sunny
Baudelaire were intelligent
children, and they were charming,
and resourceful, and had pleasant facial
features, but they were extremely unlucky, and most everything
that happened to them was rife with misfortune, misery, and despair.
I'm sorry to tell you this, but that is how the story goes.

from The Bad Beginning *by Lemony Snicket*

3 Sentence work

Lemony Snicket uses complex sentences to give the reader lots of information. One type of sentence he uses includes the relative clause, or the embedded clause.

Embedded clauses or relative clauses start with the words *that*, *which* or *who* and have a comma on either side.

For example: The thief stole a sports car. **He was dressed in a striped shirt.**

The thief, **who was dressed in a striped shirt,** stole a sports car.

Join the sentences below together to make a complex sentence with an embedded clause.

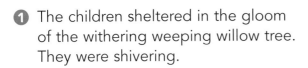

1. The queen visited the school. She was wearing her crown.

2. The tent was cold and damp. It was very old.

3. The children were fidgeting during story time. They were tired.

4. The sea was very rough on the night of the shipwreck. The sea was usually calm at that time of year.

1. The children sheltered in the gloom of the withering weeping willow tree. They were shivering.

2. The crooked tower stood on an island in the middle of a grey lake. It looked as if it was going to collapse at any moment.

3. Alex and Hardeep were exhausted by the time they reached the finish line. They had been running for over an hour.

4. The wolves were prowling at the windows of the children's railway carriage. They were crazed with hunger.

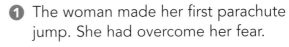

1. The woman made her first parachute jump. She had overcome her fear.

2. The snow howled and spat at the explorers as they searched for a cave to shelter them. The snow was one of the hazards of this region.

3. A flock of geese flew in formation over our house. They were migrating North.

4. The boy received the top prize in a piano competition. He has played the piano since he was four years old. The piano competition featured contestants from all over Britain.

4 Demonstration writing

You're going to write a chapter for a story using the techniques of either Jacqueline Wilson or Lemony Snicket.

Planning

Use this list to help you when planning your writing.

If you're writing in the style of **Jacqueline Wilson**, you'll need to decide:

- who will be the narrator (who is also the main character).
- what that character's dilemma or issue is and how they will reveal this.
- which other characters might be part of the dilemma.
- what will be the build-up in the chapter.

If you're writing in the style of **Lemony Snicket**, you'll need to:

- write the story from the narrator's point of view, in the third person.
- ensure the narrator's tone is serious, but the narration is witty and humorous.
- hook the reader in the first few lines.
- present the characters from the narrator's point of view, which is usually sympathetic.
- establish a strong setting by writing full descriptions
- set the plot in the real world, but exaggerate it and the characters in a humorous way.

Writing

After planning your chapter, start writing. Remember, if you are writing in the style of Jacqueline Wilson, you should use simple sentences and plenty of dialogue; if you're writing in the style of Lemony Snicket, use longer, more complex sentences.

Remember!

- Keep your author's techniques in mind while you're writing – check the list.
- Reread your work often to make sure you are still using the same techniques.
- Check that you're using the right type of sentences and language for your author's style.
- Include as much humour as your plot and author style allows.

What I have learned

- I recognise that authors use different techniques in their writing.
- I realise that author techniques can have different effects on a reader.
- I can experiment with different author techniques in my own writing.

8

The Great Debate

In this unit, you'll find out how to present two sides of an argument to use in a debate, and how to write a discussion text.

Mobile phones – good or bad?

According to the latest figures, there are over 100 million mobile phone users worldwide. The number of mobile connections is now equivalent to nearly one third of the world population, and there is an entire generation who cannot imagine life without their mobile. But are mobile phones only a good thing?

Mobile phone technology does bring benefits. In countries where land lines are difficult to lay, they enable friends and family to keep in touch. Mobile phones mean that business deals can be done on the move. We use them to call home to say we're safe, that we're going to be late or that we need a lift; moreover, we use them to summon the emergency services potentially saving precious minutes which could be spent finding a land line. Some people owe their lives to mobile phones, which, it is argued, has to make them a good thing.

Are mobile phones safe?

Yet debate still rages over mobile phone safety. Can mobile phones damage human health? Some people believe that the electromagnetic radiation emitted by the handsets causes a variety of diseases, ranging from Alzheimer's to cancer. There are also concerns that using a mobile phone can cause changes in brain activity, sleep patterns and reaction times, while research shows that using one when driving significantly increases the likelihood of traffic accidents.

A 2002 study by Finnish scientists indicated that electromagnetic radiation had an adverse effect on human brain cells in the laboratory; however the researchers downplayed the research findings, saying that further study was needed to see if the same would happen with living people. In 2004 the Karolinska Institute in Sweden carried out a study that showed that people who used a mobile phone over a period of ten years or more were four times more likely to develop ear tumours than those who had never used one. Other research has demonstrated that electromagnetic radiation affects the health of mice, but no one knows yet if this also applies to humans.

The UK government-commissioned Stewart Report, published in 2000, reported that there was no evidence to show that mobile phones had adverse health effects, but concluded that it was best to take a precautionary approach to them until more research was carried out. There is still no conclusive research, and therefore no definitive answer.

Children at risk

The report found that children are particularly vulnerable to any adverse effects that may exist. Their nervous systems are still developing, so their growing brains are more likely to absorb any radiation. It recommended that children should only use mobiles in emergencies.

In 2002 a research programme was launched, at a cost of £7.4m, jointly funded by the government and the mobile phone industry, to examine the effects of mobile phone use on health, although manufacturers continue to extol the virtues of mobiles and insist there is no evidence of risk to human health caused by their use.

It seems that, while mobile phones are here to stay, it is still sensible to minimise any potential risks by adopting some helpful strategies. Keep conversations short, make as few calls as possible, and use phones with external aerials. Hands-free kits may help since they reduce the amount of radiation to the brain.

Mobile phones – good or bad? You decide.

by Sarah Vittachi

1 Responding to the text

Read the article about mobile phone safety and answer the questions from the 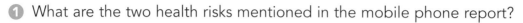, or section.

① What are the two health risks mentioned in the mobile phone report?

② What were the findings of Sweden's Karolinska Institute?

③ What advice did the Stewart Report give about the use of mobile phones?

④ Why are children said to be more at risk from mobile phone use than adults?

⑤ From reading the report, do you think that mobile phones are safe? Give two reasons for your answer.

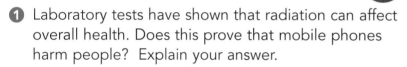

① Laboratory tests have shown that radiation can affect overall health. Does this prove that mobile phones harm people? Explain your answer.

② What were the main findings of the Stewart Report?

③ What was the aim of the £7.4m research programme set up by the government and mobile phone industry?

④ What conclusion do you think the author of the article makes? Write true or false for each of the statements below:
a) Scientific evidence proves that mobile phones are harmful to people.
b) People should ignore the studies that suggest that there are health risks caused by mobile phones.
c) Experts have recommended precautions which readers might choose to take on board.
d) Children are most at risk of damage to health and should therefore limit their use of mobile phones.

⑤ From your reading of the report, what **two** pieces of advice would you give to people buying a mobile phone?

① What benefits do mobile phones provide our culture?

② Why did scientists in Finland downplay their findings in 2002?

③ Why do you think the mobile phone industry insists that handsets are safe?

④ Summarise the conclusions of the Stewart Report.

⑤ Having read the argument, what conclusions have you drawn about the safety of mobile phones?

2 Role play

With a partner role-play the following scene:

Sam and her dad are shopping for a birthday present. Sam is trying to persuade her dad to buy her a mobile phone. But Dad has read that mobile phones might be dangerous and he's not keen. Whose argument is the strongest?

In pairs, decide who is Sam and who is Dad. Plan and rehearse your arguments. If you need to, reread the arguments in the article *Mobile phones – good or bad*?.

Remember!

- Keep in role and maintain your viewpoint.
- Listen carefully and try to present the opposite argument to your partner's.

3 Think/pair/share

Connectives are words that join two clauses together in the same sentence. In arguments, connectives are used to link ideas together to support a view.

Use the connectives in the box to create as many different logical sentences as you can by joining statements in the table with this sentence:

Children should carry mobile phones.

as	since	so that	because

Mobile phones allow children to tell their parents that they are safe.
Mobile phones may possibly harm the user's brain.
Mobile phones are expensive and make children a target for thieves.

For example: *Children should carry mobile phones since mobile phones allow children to tell their parents that they are safe.*

Use the connectives in the box to create as many different logical sentences as you can by joining ideas from the table below with one of these sentences:

Children should not use mobile phones too often.

or

Children should carry mobile phones.

| *therefore* | *although* | *however* | *since* |

| Many parents feel frightened if they don't get regular calls from their child. |
| There may be no conclusive evidence that mobile phone use causes long-term harm. |
| Children are just as safe now, without mobile phones, as children were in the past. |
| Mobile phones are expensive and make children a target for thieves. |

For example: *Although there may be no conclusive evidence that mobile phone use causes long-term harm, children should not use mobile phones too often.*

Using the connectives in the box, write down as many logical sentences as you can to show the **opposing arguments** for and against children's use of mobile phones.

You may draw from some of the arguments set out in the table below or use your own.

| *although* | *on the other hand* | *however* |

| The technology is too new for anyone to be certain of its safety. |
| No one has yet died from mobile phone use. |
| There is some research suggesting that overuse of mobile phones may harm the user's brain. |
| Many parents rely on mobile phones to keep in touch with their children. |
| Parents must weigh up the pros and cons and make up their own minds. |

For example: *No one has yet died from mobile phone use, however, many experts advise that children who have a phone should use it only in emergencies.*

4 Think/pair/share

Should children be banned from using mobile phones?

Take one side of the argument about whether children should be allowed to own mobile phones. Debate the issue with your partner, using some of these language prompts.

> In addition, research shows that …

> It is argued that …

> They believe that …

> Supporters of … say that …

> Furthermore, experts claim that …

> Overall, in my opinion …

> Some people argue that …

> There is a great deal of debate/concern about …

> On the other hand, it could be argued that …

A good sport

Research in Sweden into the effects of gaming on children's behaviour should please worried parents.

Gaming is officially good for you – in Sweden, at least. The Swedish National Institute of Public Health announced last week that playing video and computer games is not bad for children, after a growing number of anxious parents regularly turned to them for advice on its effects.

"Parents call because they are worried children are becoming increasingly violent, aggressive and overweight because of the amount of time they spend playing computer games," says Anton Lager, who, along with Sven Bremberg, investigated the effects of video and computer games on children.

In recent years, there has been a sharp increase in the popularity of computer games in Sweden. Last year, 5.6m games were sold, an on-year increase of 19.5%: that is the equivalent of every other Swede buying a computer game last year.

Kim Rydstedt, manager of Game in Täby Centrum, says: "Business is very good. Top titles like Resident Evil are always pre-booked [before their release]. There's a roaring trade in second-hand games, too."

Many parents are concerned that computer games are to blame for the escalating youth violence.

Ebba Holmberg, a 14-year-old visiting Game to pre-order a copy of Jade Empire, doesn't believe games make you violent: "They're just for fun."

Holmberg, a high-school student with plans to become a teacher, reckons games are popular "because you get involved. Anyone can be the hero, not just some Hollywood actor, like in a movie."

Eva Karlsson, 15, agrees: "It's important to have something to do on long winter nights here."

With almost 45% of Swedish homes having high-speed broadband, it is not surprising the fastest-growing sector is online gaming. A survey by Mediavision revealed 23% of Swedes used the net last month to play or download computer games.

Lager and Bremberg reviewed 30 studies from around the world that explored what effect video and computer games had on children's intelligence, aggression and weight. "We looked at how games affected spatial abilities, reaction time, aggressive play, thoughts, feelings and behaviour," says Lager.

They discovered strong evidence to suggest video and computer games are, in fact, good for you. "All the studies that looked at spatial thinking showed computer games have a positive effect," says Lager. "Playing also reduces children's reaction times."

The study discounts the link between games and violent behaviour or aggressive feelings – although a child who has been playing a violent computer game is more likely to pick up a toy sword or toy gun than a child who hasn't, according to the report.

Many Swedes were concerned about the lack of a causal link between playing computer games and obesity, but Lager is sceptical. The research he looked at suggests children only spend on average 45 minutes a day playing computer games, but more than two hours watching television. "There's been little recent research on whether the emergence of broadband and online gaming has changed this," he says.

In spite of the findings, Lager remains cautious: "Playing computer games may be good for you but too much might have an adverse effect. It's like broccoli is good for you, but 15 kilos a day probably isn't."

by Jon Buscall

Thursday April 28   *The Guardian*

5 Independent writing

Write a *Guide for Parents*, showing a balanced argument about the effects of computer games on children.

Planning your guide

First, plan the introduction. State the purpose of the guide. Note down the issue that's being debated.

Then list each argument for and against the issue. Briefly note any other useful details such as evidence to back up the argument.

Writing your guide

Write an introduction stating the purpose of the guide.

Remember!

- Use connectives to link your arguments together.

- Use extra detail and examples to support each point.

- Organise your points logically into paragraphs.

- Present both sides of the argument in a balanced way.

Use the main paragraphs to state the arguments for and against the issue, drawing on the information you've already gathered.

Add a conclusion at the end of your guide to draw the main points together.

What I have learned

- I can identify and compare viewpoints presented.

- I can argue points of view in a balanced way, both orally and in writing.

- I can retrieve information, make notes, plan and write a balanced argument.

9

Finding a Voice

In this unit, you'll read different poems about issues such as bullying and you'll compare different forms of poetry. You'll then choose an issue that's important to you and write a poem about it.

These poems are all from Cloud Busting *by Malorie Blackman.*

What's in a Name?

What's in a name? Not much.
That's what the class idiot said
After Davey's name
Was changed to Fizzy Feet.

It happened in assembly –
The second or third morning
After the long summer break,
About seven or eight months ago.

Maybe less, maybe more.
It was a long time ago,
But memories are longer.
Davey sat in front of me.

His light-brown hair
Wasn't long enough
To hide the frayed collar
Of his shirt.

His navy-blue school jumper
Had a small hole
At the elbow.
I shook my head and turned away.

My mum would never
Let me leave home
With holes at my
Elbows. No way!

Davey was the new boy,
Full of uncertain smiles
And anxious eyes
And not much else.

My best friend Alex
Sat next to me
On my right
Playing with his Gameboy.

And on my left
Alicia. A-lic-i-a!
A name like April showers
Dropping gently onto spring flowers.

(Not that I'll leave in
The bit about Alicia
When I hand this poem
To Mr Mackie. No way!)

Unit 9 Finding a Voice

Mrs Spencer, the head,
Was droning on
And on
And on …

I was sleeping
With my eyes open
When it happened.
Waking us all up.

Davey jumped up,
Fell sideways
And started rubbing his legs
Saying, "Fizzy feet! I've got fizzy feet!"

We didn't have a clue
What he was talking about.
Mr Mackie ran over
To sort him out.

"Dave, what's the matter?
What's wrong?
What's going on?"
Mr Mackie was all concern.

"Fizzy feet!
I've got fizzy feet!"
Davey pulled off his shoes
And rubbed his toes. (What a pong!)

"What're you talking about?"
Mr Mackie began to frown.
"D'you mean you've got
Pins and needles?"

"Ow! Yes, that's what I said, sir!
Fizzy feet!"
A moment's stunned silence.
Then we all roared like we had toothache.

Mr Mackie ranted
Mr Mackie raved
Mr Mackie was not happy
As he escorted Davey from the hall.

Fizzy feet,
Dizzy, fizzy feet
Busy, dizzy, fizzy feet
What a dork!

Davey never lived that down.
The class bully
Wouldn't let him.
What a dork.

Davey hated the name
Fizzy Feet
But what could he do about it?
Not much. Nothing.

The class bully wouldn't let him.

Putting the Boot In

"Pick it up,
Fizzy Feet."
Fizzy Feet
Picked it up.
"Give it here,
Fizzy Feet."
Fizzy Feet
Gave it up.
The bully despised Davey.
For a coward and a meekling.
He gave Dave so much grief and hurt.
He thought Dave was a weakling.
So whenever it would suit him
He would gladly put the boot in.

Descriptions

The class bully was
A mean, mad moron
An insane idiot
A dopey dweeb
A prize poop-head
A narrow-minded no-hoper
A hurtful, horrible person.
And everyone knew it.

The class beauty was
Alicia.
Gorgeous
A great singer
A great looker
Funny
Talented
Keen on Fizzy Feet – called him Dave.

Fizzy Feet was
Good and tall
Good and skinny
Good and quiet
A good laugh (according to Alicia)
Good at maths
Good at being friendly
Not so good with the class bully though.

1 Shared reading

Discuss the story, similes and structure of the poem *What's in a Name?*

2 Drama

Act out the scene from *What's in a Name?*

Think of a scene that might take place in the playground after the scene from *What's in a Name?* For example, your scene might explore how Davey is bullied in the playground with continued taunting and name-calling. How will you, as the children, respond to Davey? Would you intervene? Would you join in with the taunting? If you thought the bully was behaving badly, would you help Davey or not? Why?

3 Responding to the poems

Read *Putting the Boot In* and *Descriptions* from *Cloud Busting* by Malorie Blackman and answer the questions.

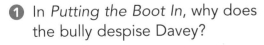

1. Why has the author chosen to set the *Putting the Boot In* in the shape of a boot?

2. Why do you think Davey does everything that the bully tells him to?

3. Write down six adjectives used to describe the class bully in *Descriptions*.

4. What are Davey's strengths?

1. In *Putting the Boot In*, why does the bully despise Davey?

2. What is the impact of listing the attributes of each person in *Descriptions*?

3. Write down examples of alliteration in *Descriptions*.

4. What does Alicia think of Davey?

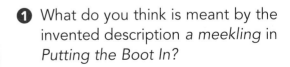

1. What do you think is meant by the invented description *a meekling* in *Putting the Boot In*?

2. What is meant by the expression *put the boot in*?

3. What do we learn about the relationship between the three characters portrayed in *Descriptions*?

4. Which of the two poems do you think is the most powerful and why?

4 Writing a poem

Beginning in the style of Malorie Blackman, write your own list poem about a bully. Add your own ideas.

The class bully was
A ...

Thinking about all the ideas you've explored during this unit, write a poem that expresses your own thoughts and feelings about an issue that's important to you.

1 Think about the sort of poem you want to write: a list poem, a shape poem or another type of poem.

2 Decide whether it'll have a patterned structure, or use a free-style structure.

3 Choose your words carefully: use powerful words and phrases that'll make an impact on the reader.

Remember!

- Keep to the structure you've chosen.

- Make sure you've expressed your thoughts and feelings about the issue in your poem.

- Try using poetic devices like alliteration, similes, metaphors and personification.

What I have learned

- I can read, respond to, analyse and evaluate poems about different issues.

- I can explore an issue that is meaningful to me and play with language to form and shape ideas that express my feelings.

- I can write a poem in response to an issue.

10

Time Travelling

In this unit, you'll read and write stories that include flashbacks, use drama to explore issues of freedom and responsibility, and you'll talk about the actions of the Suffragettes in the early twentieth century.

Maggie's Window

Maggie is a young girl living with her parents in the early twentieth century, who finds herself swept up by events.

Edith gave a sudden shout: "Police!"

Uniformed men surged out, surrounding them. In the struggle, shopping bags were kicked aside. Muriel's hat was knocked off and trodden underfoot. More people joined the watching crowd. Maggie saw Una being handcuffed, then a flash of sunlight from the spike of Dad's helmet as he turned, raising his thumb.

"We've got 'em this time," he called – and she saw Una look back at her with dawning understanding that turned to intense sad disappointment.

But Maggie hadn't betrayed them, for all her father had wanted her to. It had to be someone else.

She often looked back to that day, remembering everything that happened from the moment she first met her new companions.

⊰⋇⊱

It was raining cats and dogs and blowing a gale as Maggie came out of school. As she crossed the street, the wind scooped up a soggy piece of newspaper and plastered it against her skirt.

"You joining them bad women then, Mag?" someone shouted.

Maggie glared at the bunch of giggling girls from her school running away down the street. What bad women?

Rain trickled down her neck and the newspaper was so wet it peeled off in strips.

"WIN … ASH … LONDON … EST … END … SUFFRAG … RAMP …" was all that was left of the headlines. She rolled it into a ball and flicked the squashy mess into the gutter. Who cared what went on in London? It was like a thousand miles away. They were probably all mad and bad there.

The rain was sheeting down now. By the time she turned into the street where she lived, her boots had leaked, wetting her stockings. She went up the entry between her house and the next. Opening the door into the kitchen she heard Mam call:

"That you, our Mag? Leave your boots on, duck. I want you to take this round for me." She came into the kitchen with a packet in her hand.

"Oh, Mam, do I have to? I'm soaked."

"I promised the blouse would be ready today. Paradise Street, number 15. I've wrapped it in oilcloth. Hurry up. I'll have your tea and dry clothes ready for when you get back."

Maggie scowled, but took the packet and went out.

"Bring that oilcloth back, mind!" Mam called.

Sloshing through puddles gleaming under the gaslamps, Maggie felt as if she was in the wash tub – clothes soaked through to her vest and bloomers. The windows of the terraced houses in Paradise Street cried tears of rain. Number fifteen had light coming through thin drawn curtains. Maggie banged the knocker.

A long pause.

Losing her temper she began to bang even louder. Before she could let go, the door opened and she almost overbalanced. A face peered out.

"Yes?"

Maggie recognized the narrow green eyes and plump cheeks – Cora Carter! Not so long ago they both went to St Luke's Elementary, though Cora had been in the top class. A bossy sneak of a girl, always ready to tell on you. Maggie thrust the packet towards her.

"Mam said to bring this round – and she wants the oilcloth back." She was too fed up to care if she sounded rude.

The face retreated and there was a murmur of conversation, followed by rustling. Then the door reopened.

"You'd better come in." Cora didn't sound welcoming.

Maggie stepped straight into a small living room where three women sat around a table. Light shone from a wall gas-mantle. The table had a cloth flung untidily over it. Underneath, not quite hidden, was what looked like a strip of the calico Mam used to stiffen anything from cushion covers to jackets. Maggie saw the painted letters "VOTES FO" in green but the rest disappeared under the cloth. On the floor, as if plonked down in a rush, were some pots of paint and brushes.

"Maggie Burton, isn't it?" Cora said. "I remember you were always in hot water at school."

"I wouldn't mind some hot water now. I'm freezing." Maggie hadn't meant to joke and the sudden laughter made her feel silly.

"Put the kettle on for some tea, Edith," one of the women said. "We all need warming."

Edith, big and bony, jumped up, kicking over a pot of green paint with one large foot. A brush shot onto the cloth and paint splashed both calico and the older woman's shoes.

"I'm so sorry, Muriel. All our work for nothing. The lettering is ruined … what a blithering idiot!"

"Never mind that." Muriel patted her grey bun of hair, with a warning glance towards Maggie. "See to your friend, Cora."

Cora frowned and flushed. Unwrapping the wet oilcloth she shoved it at Maggie. "Tell your mam I'll be round Friday with the money."

An awkwardness filled the room. The third woman, a skinny red-head with a snub nose, fetched cloths and a basin of water. Mopping the floor, she gave Maggie a quick smile. There was no offer of tea, but Maggie was only too glad to escape into the street, despite the sleet.

Once home, she changed and wolfed down the sausages and mash left in the oven to keep warm. Her dad, back from his shift at the station, was toasting his feet on the fender as he read his newspaper. He turned a page and shook it.

Maggie saw the headlines …

"MASS WINDOW SMASHING IN LONDON'S WEST END. SUFFRAGETTES ON THE RAMPAGE!" So that's what her schoolmates were on about!

"What's Suffragettes, Dad?"

"Eh?" He looked to see what she had been reading. "Oh, them! A bunch of loonies. Nothing worth bothering with. Pour us some more tea, duck."

She did as he asked and passed him his cup. "What do they do?"

"What do who do?" Mam asked, coming downstairs.

Maggie pointed to the newspaper headline.

"Crack-brained women as want their heads looking at!" Mam said with a disapproving sniff. "Breaking folk's windows … burning buildings. All for some daft notion about being like men so as they can vote who goes to Parliament."

Hearing "VOTE" was like a firecracker going off. Big green letters seemed to dance in the air in front of Maggie's eyes. Cora and those others with their calico and pots of paint – were they Suffragettes?

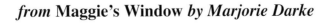

Mam was still talking. "They'll end up in jug, the lot of 'em, and good riddance!" She began to clear the table.

from **Maggie's Window** *by Marjorie Darke*

1 Responding to the texts

Read the passage from the short story, *Maggie's Window*, and then answer the questions. The story opens with a glimpse of the final scene. The rest of the story is then told in flashback.

1. Who are the *uniformed men* referred to in the second line?

2. What does Maggie's father think about Suffragettes?

3. Why were women breaking windows and burning buildings?

4. What do you think Cora and her friends were doing with the pots of paint?

1. What do we learn about Maggie's father in the opening scene?

2. Why do you think Una looks at Maggie with *intense sad disappointment*?

3. What does Maggie's mother think about Suffragettes?

4. What do you think Maggie's mother means when she says, *They'll end up in jug*?

1. We find out in the opening scene that one of Maggie's female companions will be arrested. Why do you think the author reveals this so early in the story?

2. What questions does the author leave unanswered in the opening scene?

3. What does the newspaper heading tell us about the Suffragettes and the news reporter's attitude towards them?

4. How do you think the Suffragettes would have defended their actions?

2 Shared reading

Read and discuss this report in *The Morning Post* newspaper from June 1914.

Arrested at Buckingham Palace

Four militant Suffragists appeared at the main gates of Buckingham Palace yesterday afternoon. One of them chained herself to the gates, while another waved a flag and shouted. When these two were taken to Cannon-row Police Station their two companions accompanied them and waited at the station till informed that their friends would probably be brought up at Bow-street today.

3 Independent note-making

Find information in your class library or on the Internet to answer these questions.

1 In what year were women over the age of 30 able to vote?

2 What is significant about the colours green, white and purple?

3 In what year were women granted equal voting rights to men?

4 Independent writing

1 Read the report *Arrested at Buckingham Palace* from *The Morning Post* newspaper in 1914 on page 69.

2 Write a story based on the event outlined in the report. Imagine you were there. Begin your story a few years later, at a time when women over the age of 30 were allowed to vote in Britain. You could begin like this:

I watch as my mother climbs the steps of the Town Hall, proudly clutching a brooch adorned with a white pearl surrounded by violet and emerald stones: white for purity, purple for dignity and green for hope. The brooch is damaged; its pin snapped clean off when it was trodden underfoot during the chaotic scene outside the gates of Buckingham Palace, just five years ago. I was there.

Remember!

- Think about how you'll use time in your story.

- Include a flashback to draw the reader back in time to a significant event.

- Check that the details in your story are historically accurate; for example don't refer to mobile phones, trainers or email.

VOTE TODAY

I watch as my mother proudly climbs the steps to vote in a local election for the first time. Today she beams at me with satisfaction but she wasn't smiling back then, in the summer of 1914. She sees me now but she didn't see me then, outside the Palace gates. She didn't know I was watching her that day but I saw. I saw what happened …

3 Continue the story. Describe the events of June 1914 in a flashback. What were the characters in your story doing at the time? Why were they outside the gates of Buckingham Palace?

What I have learned

- I can write a short story that uses time in an interesting way.

- I can use research to support the details in my story writing.

11

Walk to School

In this unit, you'll read different types of non-fiction texts that use formal and impersonal language to complain, inform, explain and persuade. Then you'll plan and write a non-fiction text of your own to present information for a website or brochure.

First Walking Bus launched in Sittingbourne

It was a proud moment for Bobbing Village School when pupils stepped out to join the Kent Walking Bus for the first time.

The Bobbing School Walking Bus is launched.

Their journey was especially important as Bobbing School's Walking Bus is the first to be launched in Sittingbourne and the Mayor and Lady Mayoress visited the school to mark the special occasion.

In warm autumn sunshine, 12 pupils happily donned their hi-viz Walking Bus tabards and began a 25-minute stroll to school from the Meads Estate, along Quinton Road and into Sheppey Way taking them all the way to the school gates.

Walking Bus Co-ordinator Mrs Nicky Chambers, who is mother of Year Three pupil Harry, seven, said: "Harry was so excited, he absolutely loved the walk, and he especially liked wearing his new Walking Bus tabard. All the children enjoyed themselves and we even made up our own Walking Bus song which we chanted along the way."

The pupils took part in a special ceremony held at the school, where Bobbing head teacher Mrs Katrina Ware presented them each with a certificate to mark their achievement.

A buffet was laid on for the occasion and fine food was enjoyed by the many sponsors and supporters of the Walking Bus who attended the event.

Deputy head teacher Mrs Lois Hudson said: "We launched the Walking Bus to help ease the traffic congestion outside the school, which is something all schools suffer from. It is also part of our Healthy Schools Initiative to encourage more children to walk to school. The day has been perfect and it has been a very successful launch indeed."

1 Responding to the text

Answer questions from the , or section.

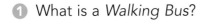

1. What is a *Walking Bus*?

2. How long does it take pupils to walk from the Meads Estate to their school gates?

3. At what time of year did this event take place?

4. Who were the guests of honour at this special occasion?

5. Why do you think the Mayor and Mayoress attended the event?

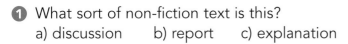

1. What sort of non-fiction text is this?
   a) discussion   b) report   c) explanation

2. How did the school celebrate the launch of the Walking Bus?

3. Write a list of positive words and phrases used in the report.

4. How does the photograph help you to understand the news report?

5. Think of a new heading for the report.

1. *Pupils happily donned their hi-viz Walking Bus tabards.* What does the reporter mean by this?

2. What are the advantages of the Walking Bus scheme according to the deputy head teacher?

3. What other advantages can you think of?

4. What role do you think the *sponsors and supporters* played in making the Walking Bus a success?

5. In what ways has the event been a *very successful launch*?

Walking Buses

The website articles describe the benefits of Walking Buses.

Hop on board the Walking Bus

Traffic congestion, particularly in the streets surrounding our schools, is a problem that requires action by the community if it is to be tackled effectively.

One excellent way you can make a difference is to support the operation of a Walking Bus to your local primary school.

Walking Buses improve the health of the children using them, teach them vital road safety skills, save parents' time and reduce traffic congestion and pollution in the streets around the school.

What is a Walking Bus?

Walking Buses are organised walks to school. "Buses" operate along set routes, picking up children at pre-arranged points. Everyone involved wears high-visibility tabards and baseball caps provided free by our project. Adults involved are police-checked and routes approved by the council. Because of concerns over obesity levels in children and their lack of road safety skills, as well as the issue of growing traffic congestion, Walking Buses are attracting considerable interest from government.

What's in it for us?

Walking Buses are a great way for children to travel safely, healthily and enjoyably to school. We need the support of local businesses to ensure that more and more children can benefit from the choice of a Walking Bus to take them to school, and that communities can benefit from the positive effects that these resources can have on road safety awareness among children, as well as health and the environment.

from www.kentwalkingbus.org

What do you think of the walking bus?

"I like it because it makes me really hungry, then I get home and eat all my tea. If I eat all my tea up I usually get pudding." Peter, aged 7

"I think it's a good idea because it gets people to stop using their cars and I hate the noise they make and the stinkfumes." Katie, aged 5

from www.foe.co.uk

2 Independent writing

Read *Hop on board the Walking Bus*. The information is taken from a website explaining what a Walking Bus is, how the scheme operates and how it benefits the community.

Think about …

- the problem identified in the opening sentence.

- the use of persuasive language.

- the benefits that are outlined.

- the question and answer format.

Write an information text for a website or brochure explaining how a Walking Bus operates. Use the information in *Hop on board the Walking Bus* as a starting point.

Or, think of another idea of your own to help solve a problem in your area.

Remember!

- Outline the problems that your idea can help to overcome.

- Explain how your idea works.

- Use persuasive language.

What I have learned

- I understand how non-fiction information can be presented in a number of formats for different purposes and audiences.

- I can research and assemble information from different sources.

- I can plan a presentation of non-fiction information that combines writing with different modes of communication.

12

Plays and Performance

In this unit, you'll read and perform a scene from a Shakespeare play and a modern play, and write a play scene of your own.

Macbeth and the Witches

As predicted by three witches, Macbeth has become King of Scotland by murdering the previous king. He has also murdered his friend, Banquo. Greatly troubled by nightmares, he revisits the witches to find out what is in store for him. The witches cast a spell, conjuring up infernal spirits to reveal the future.

In a dark cave, filled with the stench from a bubbling cauldron, the three witches sat making black magic. Flesh from snakes, frogs, bats and worms; organs from dogs, lizards, tigers and murdered men – they all plopped into the stinking brew. And blood, of course, always blood. The night was so thick with sinister magic that Hecate herself, Queen of Witches, joined in preparing the wicked spells.

For all the stink, the crones still sensed when Macbeth was close by – he reeked so of evil. They were

expecting him, too. He came
ravenous for answers, wanting the
darkest secrets from the pit of hell.
Accordingly, they raised for him
apparitions from the seething cauldron,
the steam shaping itself first into a visored helmet,
then a bloodstained child, then a baby in a crown.
The apparitions warned him to beware Macduff. But they urged him to
press on along the course he had begun, fearlessly, since no man born of
woman would ever kill him, and no rebellion would ever defeat him until
the day Birnam Wood marched on the Castle of Dunsinane.

"Well, what wood ever walked, and what man was ever born except
by a woman? I am invincible! This is what I came here to hear!
Before I go, though ..."

"Ask no more," warned the witches.

"But I must know. The rest is useless without it. Will Banquo's heirs
ever be kings now that he's dead? Show me the truth!"

Not one apparition, but eight, came in answer to his demand. They came,
conjured from the smoke – seven identical images of crowned boys, and lastly
Banquo holding up a mirror in which were reflected countless more sons. The
descendants of Banquo would, it seemed, rule over Scotland for
centuries.

"Why so miserable, Macbeth?" cackled the witches, and
danced for him, a grisly, grinning dance like tormented souls
writhing in hellfire. Then they disappeared, as if they had
never been.

from Macbeth *retold by Geraldine McCaughrean*

1 Responding to the text

Answer the questions from the , or 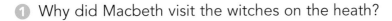 section.

1. Why did Macbeth visit the witches on the heath?

2. What did the witches put in the *stinking brew*?

3. What was it like in the dark cave? How does the author use the sense of smell in her language to develop the setting?

4. What are apparitions? Use a dictionary if you need to.

5. Do you think Macbeth should trust the witches? Give reasons for your answer.

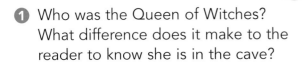

1. Who was the Queen of Witches? What difference does it make to the reader to know she is in the cave?

2. What did Macbeth want to find out from the witches?

3. What apparitions were shown to Macbeth?

4. How does the author use language to develop a sense of evil in the cave?

5. Did the witches put Macbeth's mind at rest?

1. The author writes that Macbeth *came ravenous for answers*. What does this mean?

2. Why does Macbeth believe he is invincible?

3. Why was Macbeth so miserable at the end of his visit to the witches?

4. How does the author show the reader that the witches are enjoying his misery?

5. What do you think Macbeth should do when he leaves the cave? Do you think he will do it? Give reasons for your answers.

The Surprise Birthday Party

After their father mysteriously disappears, Bobbie, Phyllis and Peter move to a small cottage in the countryside. They spend a lot of time at the railway station and make friends with the stationmaster, Mr Perks. When they find out it is Mr Perks' birthday the children decide to tell everyone in the village and collect gifts in a pram for a surprise birthday party at his house. The children hide in the next room as Perks enters the parlour. He finds the pram full of presents.

❖

(Sheepishly, Roberta, Peter and Phyllis enter.)

Phyllis: Oh Mr Perks, I thought you'd be pleased.

Perks: Pleased? When have I ever complained of being short of anything? Eh? Tell me that.

Roberta: You've not, Mr Perks, but they're presents and people give presents on birthdays, what's wrong with that?

Perks: Nowt's wrong with it. A present. One present – but when you've got heaps and heaps of 'em. Like this …

Peter: But they're not all from us.

Perks: Oh no?

Roberta: They're from all sorts of people in the village only we forgot to put labels on.

Perks: People from the village?

Peter: Yes.

Perks: They've never given me presents afore so who put 'em up to it?

Phyllis: *(all innocent)* Why, we did, of course.

Perks: Well that is marvellous. That is blinking marvellous. So you've been round telling the neighbours we can't make both ends meet?

Mrs Perks: I'm sure they didn't mean it, Albert.

Peter: No, we didn't.

Perks: Whether they meant it or not they did it. How can I hold me head up in the village now after this lot?

Phyllis: I thought we were friends.

Perks: So did I! I don't call this no friendship, showing me up like this.

Roberta: Oh we didn't mean it, honestly we didn't.

Peter: We didn't.

Phyllis: Honestly.

(The children start to cry.)

Mrs Perks: Now look what you've done.

Perks: Serves 'em right.

Mrs Perks: I hope you're satisfied.

Roberta: *(through her tears)* But you've got it all wrong, Mr Perks.

Perks: Oh, have I indeed?

Roberta: People gave you these presents not from charity but because they liked you.

Perks: Oh yeah? I bet!

78

Roberta: If you won't even listen!

Perks: To what?

Mrs Perks: You are a stubborn old fool sometimes, Albert Perks. Why don't you listen for once in your life?

Perks: Huh!

Roberta: All I wanted to say was that – was that – well – everyone – who gave you a present passed on a message to you.

Perks: Huh!

Mrs Perks: Go on, love, he's listening.

Roberta: These are clothes from Mother for your youngest. Mother said, "I'll find some of Phyllis' things that she's grown out of if you're quite sure Mr Perks wouldn't be offended and think it's meant for charity. I'd like to do some little thing for him because he's been so kind to you. I can't do much because we're poor ourselves."

Mrs Perks: You see, Albert!

Perks: Your mam's a born lady, I'll give her that. All right, we'll keep the clothes.

Roberta: Then there's the perambulator and the gooseberries from Mrs Ransome. She said, "I dare say the Perks' children'd like these gooseberries." And she told me to tell you the pram was her little Emma's who died after six months and she'd like to see it used.

Mrs Perks: Oh, I can't send the pram back, Albert.

Perks: Am I asking you to?

Roberta: Then the shovel. Mr James made it for you himself, and he said, "You tell Mr Perks it's a pleasure to make a little thing for a man what is much respected."

Perks: I suppose James is a good enough fellah.

Roberta: Then the honey and the bootlaces. Mr James said he respected a man who paid his way – and the butcher said the same. And the old turnpike woman said many was the time you'd lent her a hand with her garden when you were a lad – and things like that came home to roost – I don't know what she meant. And everybody who gave you anything said they liked you, and it was a very good idea of ours and nobody said anything about charity or anything horrid like that and I thought you'd love to know how fond people are of you and I never was so unhappy in all my life. So good-bye. I hope you'll forgive us some day. *(Turning to the others)* Come on, let's go home.

Perks: Now hold on a sec.

Mrs Perks: I should think so too.

(The children, still rather tearful, turn.)

**from The Railway Children
adapted by Dave Simpson**

2 Responding to the text

Answer the questions from the , or section.

❶ Is Mr Perks poor or rich? How do you know?

❷ Make a list of the presents Mr Perks receives on his birthday.

❸ Why are James and the butcher happy to give Mr Perks presents?

❹ The stage directions say the children are tearful. Why is this an important stage direction?

❺ What are Mr Perks' feelings when he begins to listen to Roberta? What are his feelings at the end?

❻ Roberta thinks she has acted like a friend. How much do you think she has acted as a friend?

❶ Who are the two main characters in this scene? What does Mrs Perks do in the scene? Why has the playwright included her?

❷ What does Roberta do to convince Mr Perks that they had done the right thing by giving him presents?

❸ One of the themes of the scene is respect. Does Mr Perks feel he is respected at the beginning? Does he change his mind? Why do you think this?

❹ Perks says *Now hold on a sec* at the end. Write a stage direction for this line and explain why you have chosen it.

❺ Later, Mr Perks says, *If a man can't respect hisself then no one else'll respect him neither*. What does this tell you about the reasons he was angry?

❻ How do you think Roberta feels: a) when Mr Perks is angry with her at the beginning b) after she reads out the messages c) when Mr Perks says *Now hold on a sec*?

❶ Was it a good idea for Roberta to write down what the neighbours said when they gave the presents? Why?

❷ Look at what the old turnpike woman said. What does this mean and what does it tell us about Mr Perks when he was a boy?

❸ Identify two stage directions that help the actors to perform the script and say how these stage directions help them.

❹ How does Mr Perks think the neighbours feel about him by the end of the scene?

❺ Is Mr Perks wrong to be angry? Explain your answer.

❻ One of the themes of this scene is friendship. How does Mr Perks feel about his friendship with the children at first and at the end?

3 Grammar work

Answer the questions from the , or section.

Copy out the playscript lines below. In the **stage directions** underline any adverbs or adverbial phrases in red and any verbs in blue.

1. **Roberta:** *(loudly)* Look! There is a huge mound of rock and earth on the railway line.

2. **Peter:** *(gazing down the track)* The 11.29 train hasn't gone by yet. We must let them know at the station.

3. **Roberta:** We haven't got time to run there. We have to think of something else. *(in deep thought)*

4. **Peter:** *(frantically searching)* Couldn't we make a flag or something to warn the driver?

5. **Phyllis:** *(hopping from foot to foot nervously)* But we haven't got anything red. I'm scared.

Remember!

- If it tells you what to do it's a **verb**.

- If it tells you how, when or where to do it, it's an **adverb** or an **adverbial phrase**.

Copy out these lines and add your own stage directions using verbs, adverbs and adverbial phrases.

1. **Peter:** Shut up! Stop being a baby.

2. **Roberta:** Stop fighting you two. I've got an idea! We could use some material from my flannel petticoat. It's red.

3. **Phyllis:** Here, Bobbie. You can use these sticks. They should be long enough for flags.

4. **Peter:** Well done, Phyl! It won't take me a minute to tie the red material to the sticks.

5. **Roberta:** There's just one thing. We'll have to stand next to the track if the driver is to have any chance of seeing us in time.

6. **Phyllis:** We have to do it. We have to save the passengers on the train. Come on! I'm going down to the track.

Read the dialogue in the and activities. Write an ending to the scene, with stage directions.

4 Independent writing

You're going to write a play scene that develops to a dramatic moment.

Planning

Discuss your ideas and plan the main points of the scene. Spend some time thinking about this and check it'll work on an audience by discussing it with a partner.

Writing

Start writing your script and read back your lines to yourself often so that you can hear what it sounds like. Use stage directions to guide your actors.

Editing

Reread your script and look carefully for these points:

1 Put the speakers' names in bold or underline them.

2 Start each new speaker's speech on a new line, for example:

Katie: Give me back my ball.

Ben: No I won't.

3 Don't use speech marks.

4 Don't use speech verbs, for example *said* or *yelled*.

5 Put stage directions in brackets.

Remember!

- Create one main character that the audience cares about

- Give the main character a problem.

- Give information to the audience through the dialogue.

- Give information to the actor through the stage directions.

- Read aloud as you write to check how it'll sound to an audience.

What I have learned

- I understand the differences between writing a narrative and a play.

- I can identify the main themes in a play scene and how dramatic tension is developed.

- I can write a script for a play scene, and understand how to shape it for an audience.

Revision: Fiction

13

In this unit, you'll practise answering questions about fiction texts and revise the writing skills needed for writing fiction.

1 Independent writing

You've 20 minutes to plan and write this text. Aim to spend about five minutes on your planning and the rest of the time on your writing. Remember to leave a few minutes at the end of the task to check your writing.

Imagine you arrive at school to find your regular teacher has been replaced for the day by a very unusual supply teacher. Write a short story about a part of the day describing the teacher and their unusual ways of teaching.

Use paragraphs when the speaker changes, and when something new happens, such as a change in time and place.

Good morning class

Remember!

- Focus on one or two striking details of the teacher.
- Use dialogue to move the story along and to tell the reader something about the character.
- Choose your verbs thoughtfully as they give your story power, for example, use **hobbled** rather than **walked**.

2 Independent writing

You've 20 minutes to plan and write this text. Aim to spend about five minutes on your planning and the rest of the time on your writing. Remember to leave a few minutes at the end to check your writing.

Imagine you're moving to a new house. On your first day, you discover a hidden door. Write about what happens when you go through the door. What will you find there?

Try to use a range of sentence types.

Remember!

- Use your *senses* to describe the setting – tell the reader about what is seen, heard and smelt.

- Focus sharply on a few details.

- Choose the *best* adjectives for the job, and take time to think about them.

- Proofread your work. Is the punctuation correct? Read your writing back to yourself. Do sentences have full stops and capital letters? Do they make sense? Do they give the information the reader needs?

3 Write/pair/share

In pairs, write a story plan for the title *The Stranger*.

You can choose a genre for your story. Remember to spend about 10 or 15 minutes on your planning.

Remember!

- Think who your audience is.
- Choose an interesting and intriguing main character.
- Work out the plot. Does your story build to a climax? Use an excitement graph to help you. Briefly note down the most important events that happen to your character.
- Note how the character responds to the events in the story plan.
- Keep it simple.

Use features of your chosen genre, for example, the style of settings, characters and plot. Plan a strong ending for your story. Open in a way that grabs the reader's interest.

4 Independent writing

You've 45 minutes to plan and write this text. Aim to spend about 10 or 15 minutes on your planning and the rest of the time on your writing. Remember to leave a few minutes at the end of the task to check your writing.

Read the article about the wolf. Imagine you're either the wolf or the child. Write the story of the wolf's escape and capture from your point of view.

Escaped wolf found in shed

An old wolf escaped from a popular wildlife park on Friday night. She was seen loping through the small town of Oakingham at dawn early on Saturday morning and was found later in the day in a shed in the back garden of one of the houses. The wolf was with a child of primary school age at the time.

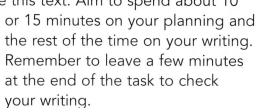

Remember!

- Think of something to say and a voice to say it in, for example first person or third person.

- Plan how you want to say it, for example by using a story mountain.

- Use a variety of interesting sentences, for example simple, compound and complex sentences.

- Choose the most effective vocabulary to make the sentences lively, for example powerful verbs, adverbials of time, similes and metaphors.

- Tie sentences together into paragraphs with connectives.

- Link paragraphs together so they build up towards the ending.

- Read your work back to yourself as if you are the reader. Be your own critic.

What I have learned

- I can plan a piece of fiction, taking into account the genre and my audience.

- I can write a piece of short and longer fiction, using simple, compound and complex sentences.

- I can include powerful vocabulary and imagery in my writing.

14

Revision: Non-fiction

In this unit, you'll practise answering questions about non-fiction texts and revise the writing skills needed for writing different types of non-fiction.

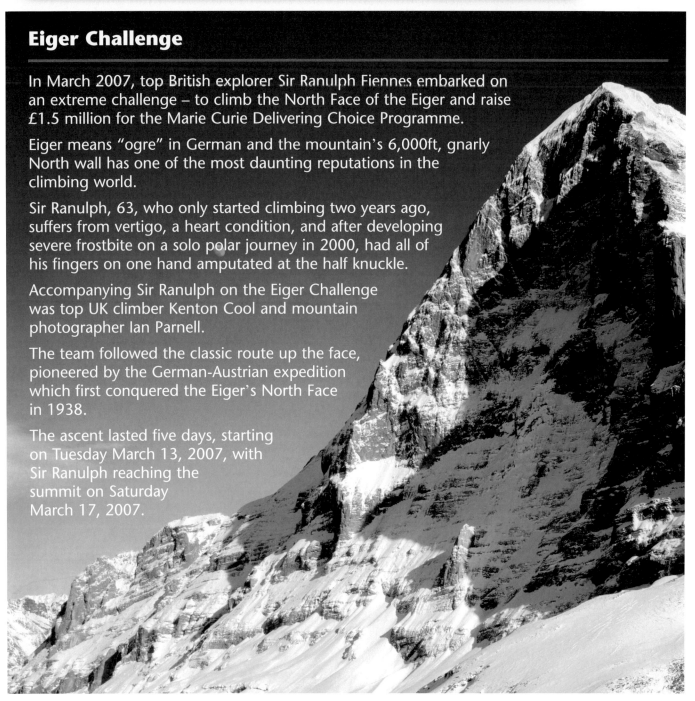

Eiger Challenge

In March 2007, top British explorer Sir Ranulph Fiennes embarked on an extreme challenge – to climb the North Face of the Eiger and raise £1.5 million for the Marie Curie Delivering Choice Programme.

Eiger means "ogre" in German and the mountain's 6,000ft, gnarly North wall has one of the most daunting reputations in the climbing world.

Sir Ranulph, 63, who only started climbing two years ago, suffers from vertigo, a heart condition, and after developing severe frostbite on a solo polar journey in 2000, had all of his fingers on one hand amputated at the half knuckle.

Accompanying Sir Ranulph on the Eiger Challenge was top UK climber Kenton Cool and mountain photographer Ian Parnell.

The team followed the classic route up the face, pioneered by the German-Austrian expedition which first conquered the Eiger's North Face in 1938.

The ascent lasted five days, starting on Tuesday March 13, 2007, with Sir Ranulph reaching the summit on Saturday March 17, 2007.

from **www.mariecurie.org.uk**

Sir Ranulph Fiennes' Account

I'm 63 years old. I'm terrified of heights. I've had a double heart bypass. This March I will be climbing the North Face of the Eiger. Why? Well, I've been an explorer for more than 25 years, but this is my challenge of a lifetime. The North Face is 6,000ft of vertical rock and ice. It's claimed the lives of 50 climbers since the first ascent in 1938 and is notorious for rockfalls, avalanches and unstable weather.

But I'm determined to get to the top – vertigo and all. I'm taking on the Eiger Challenge not just "because it's there" but to raise £1.5 million to support the pioneering work of Marie Curie Cancer Care's Delivering Choice Programme.

The Eiger is a big monster, but it's the knowledge that Marie Curie Cancer Care will benefit from my efforts that makes contemplating this huge personal challenge easier.

from **www.myspace.com/ranulphfiennes**

1 Role play

In pairs, role-play an interview with Sir Ranulph Fiennes or another mountaineer for a radio or television show.

Before you begin, think about:

* what motivates someone to take on such a challenge.
* how they might prepare for the challenge.
* what they'd take with them.

2 Responding to the text

Read the two non-fiction texts carefully. Then answer the following questions.

1. What is Sir Ranulph Fiennes most famous for? [1 mark]
2. Who accompanied Sir Ranulph Fiennes on a polar journey in 2000? [1 mark]
3. Why did Sir Ranulph Fiennes decide to climb the North Face of the Eiger? [2 marks]
4. Why do you think the mountain was named *Eiger*, meaning *ogre*? [1 mark]
5. In what year was the Eiger first conquered? [1 mark]
6. What geographical conditions make the Eiger particularly difficult for climbers? [3 marks]
7. What health problems made the climb even more of a challenge for Sir Ranulph Fiennes? [3 marks]

3 Independent writing

You've 20 minutes to plan and write this task. Aim to spend about five minutes on your planning and the rest of the time on your writing. Remember to leave a few minutes at the end of the task to check your writing.

Write a recount about a recent challenge.

Choose one of the following options:
a) Imagine you're a mountaineer and write about a recent challenge.
b) Write about a recent challenge you've faced in real life.

In your plan, think about these questions:

- What was the challenge?
- What made you take on the challenge?
- How did you prepare yourself?
- Did you successfully complete the challenge?

Living with Volcanoes

About five hundred million people, or one in ten of the world's population, live in places that are at risk from volcanoes. Their homes could be hit by lava flows, pyroclastic flows or mud flows. Many live on old lava flows and in valleys that have been swept by mud flows or pyroclastic flows in the past.

Cities at risk

Naples in Italy could be affected by pyroclastic flows from a major eruption of Vesuvius. Parts of Seattle in the USA could be swamped by mud flows if Mount Rainier explodes like Mount St Helens did. These risks were not known when these cities were founded and as they developed. It would be impossible to relocate the cities now.

Volcanic soil

Millions of people live near volcanoes because there is nowhere else for them to live. Others choose to take a risk because volcanoes produce fertile soil and are good places to farm.

The soil on the lower slopes of volcanoes is made from eroded lava and ash. It is full of minerals that plants need to grow, which makes it excellent for growing crops. Many huge coffee plantations are located on volcanoes in Central America, for example, and there are many vineyards around Mount Vesuvius. Farmers often return to volcanic slopes even after their farms have been destroyed by eruptions, because the soil is so rich.

There are other advantages to living near volcanoes. Volcanic rocks make good building materials. Lava and tuff can be sawn into building blocks, and cinders are used on the surface of paths and roads. The heat from hot rocks in volcanic areas is used to heat water and to generate electricity.

Ploughing fields in the shadow of Mayon, an active volcano in the Philippines. The rich volcanic soil is good for growing crops, but the fields could be swept away by pyroclastic flows.

These children live near the Sakurajima volcano in Japan. They always wear helmets on the way to and from school to protect them from rocks hurled out by eruptions.

CASE STUDY

Farming on Mayon

The Mayon volcano in the Philippines has a major eruption about every ten years, sending out ash columns, pyroclastic flows and mud flows. There is not much farming land in the area, so farmers grow rice, coconut palms and vegetables on Mayon's slopes. But it is a risky way to live. Tragically, seventy-five farmers were killed during an eruption in 1993.

from **Nature's Fury: Volcano!** *by Anita Ganeri*

4 Responding to the text

Read *Living with Volcanoes* carefully. Then answer the following questions.

1. Name two cities that could be affected by volcanic eruptions in the future. [2 marks]

2. What reasons are given to explain why people are living near to dangerous volcanoes? [3 marks]

3. Why do children living near the Sakurajima volcano in Japan wear helmets on the way to and from school? [1 mark]

4. What is *tuff*? [1 mark]
   a) Lava   b) Volcanic rock   c) Building bricks

5. How would scientists classify the Mayon volcano in the Philippines? [1 mark]
   a) Active   b) Dormant   c) Extinct

6. Why do you think farmers continue living and working on the slopes of the Mayon volcano? [2 marks]

5 Independent writing

You've 45 minutes to plan and write this text. Aim to spend about 10 or 15 minutes on your planning and the rest of the time on your writing. Remember to leave a few minutes at the end of the task to check your writing.

Write a discussion text exploring the reasons why people live on or near to volcanoes.

Remember!

- Begin by making a statement about the issue you'll be discussing.

- Explore both the benefits and the risks of living near a volcano.

- State what needs to be done to help reduce the risks.

What I have learned

- I can recall the language and organisational features of different non-fiction text types.

- I understand how to approach reading a non-fiction text.

- I am aware of a range of questions and how to answer them, and can improve my own answers.

- I can write non-fiction effectively for a particular purpose and audience, drawing on different language and organisational features.

15

Revision: Poetry

In this unit, you'll practise reading poems and answering questions about them.

The Fly

How large unto the tiny fly
Must little things appear! –
A rosebud like a feather bed,
Its prickle like a spear;

A dewdrop like a looking-glass,
A hair like golden wire;
The smallest grain of mustard-seed
As fierce as coals of fire;

A loaf of bread, a lofty hill;
A wasp, a cruel leopard;
And specks of salt as bright to see
As lambkins to a shepherd.

Walter de la Mare

A Fly and a Flea in a Flue

A fly and a flea in a flue
Were imprisoned, so what could they do?
Said the fly, "Let us flee!"
"Let us fly!" said the flea,
So they flew through a flaw in the flue.

P. L. Mannock

1 Responding to the poems

Read both poems carefully. Then answer the questions.

Questions 1–4 are about *The Fly*.

1 What is the first poem about? [2 marks]

2 What simile does the poet use to describe how the thorn of a rose must appear to a fly? [1 mark]

3 Find and write another simile the poet has used in the first verse. [1 mark]

4 What words has the poet used to refer to size and scale? [3 marks]

Questions 5–8 are about *A Fly and a Flea in a Flue*.

5 What sort of poem is *A Fly and a Flea in a Flue*? [1 mark]
   a) Riddle   b) Limerick   c) Haiku   d) Tanka

6 *Flea* and *flee* are homophones. Find and write down another pair of homophones in the poem. [1 mark]

7 What is a flue? [1 mark]
   a) An illness   b) A liquid   c) A slide   d) A tube or pipe

8 Find six alliterative words and write them down. [2 marks]

Five Eyes

In Hans' old Mill his three black cats
Watch his bins for the thieving rats.
Whisker and claw, they crouch in the night,
Their five eyes smouldering green and bright:
Squeaks from the flour sacks, squeaks from where
The cold wind stirs on the empty stair,
Squeaking and scampering, everywhere.
Then down they pounce, now in, now out,
At whisking tail, and sniffing snout;
While lean old Hans he snores away
Till peep of light at break of day;
Then up he climbs to his creaking mill,
Out come his cats all grey with meal –
Jekkel, and Jessup, and one-eyed Jill.

Walter de la Mare

Leopard

Gentle hunter
His tail plays on the ground
While he crushes the skull.

Beautiful death
Who puts on a spotted robe
When he goes to his victim.

Playful killer
Whose loving embrace
Splits the antelope's heart.

a Yoruba poem

2 Responding to the poems

Read both poems carefully. Then answer the following questions.

Questions 1–5 are about *Five Eyes*.

1 Describe the setting for this poem as fully as you can, using words from the text. [2 marks]

2 What do you think the rats that come into the mill are looking for? [1 mark]

3 Write down words and phrases the poet has used to describe the noise and chaos that takes place while Hans is sleeping. [2 marks]

4 What is the name of the cat with one eye? [1 mark]

5 Find and write an example of alliteration in the poem. [1 mark]

Questions 6–9 are about *Leopard*.

6 What is the hunter's victim in *Leopard*? [1 mark]

7 Why do you think the poet chose the phrases *Gentle hunter* and *Playful killer* to describe the leopard? Refer to other lines in the poem to support your answer. [2 marks]

8 Explain the reference to *a spotted robe* in the second part of the poem. [1 mark]

9 In the third part of the poem, what metaphor does the poet use to describe the act of killing? [1 mark]

Remember!

- Try to answer all of the questions, taking care not to miss any out.

- Note the key words in each question and make sure you understand what is being asked.

- Check to see how many marks each question is worth.

- Read through your answers at the end making sure you have answered the questions as fully as possible.

What I have learned

- I can read and analyse different types of poetry, taking into account the main literary features.

- I can read and respond to poems confidently in a test situation.